Body La

Body language

Published by
Lotus Press

Body Language

S. Kant

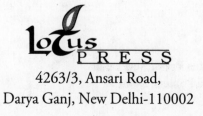

4263/3, Ansari Road,
Darya Ganj, New Delhi-110002

LOTUS PRESS

4263/3, Ansari Road, Darya Ganj, New Delhi- 110002

Ph.: 32903912, 23280047 • E-mail : lotus_press@sify.com

www.lotuspress.co.in

Body Language

© 2011, Lotus Press

ISBN: 81-8382-175-8

Published by : **Lotus Press,** New Delhi

Printed at : Chetna Printers, Delhi

PREFACE

Humans live within the reality of their bodies; eating, sleeping, playing and working. Their emotions are enmeshed in nearly every social interaction, whether it is a goodbye wave of the hand or a complex set of interactions, as in sports activities or orchestral performances. At festive activities, humans share their emotions with others, ritualistically and contagiously, cheering on their team, shouting at the other team, moving in unison in a great wave of collective body motion. People feel happy at weddings; they feel sad at funerals. They display their emotions, which tell others how they feel.

There are several ways of displaying the emotions and communicating with each other. Apart from verbal communication, the nonverbal communication or simply known as the body language is one of the strongest medium of giving messages without uttering a single word. Strong and effective body language can win people but on the other hand weak body language can send negative signals even when the person is not so weak otherwise.

The study of nonverbal communication *(Body Language)* continues to grow across the spectrum of research in many fields of study. The present book is also written keeping the ever growing importance of body language across the sectors in mind. We have tried to give the various aspects of body language in this book in a very pragmatic and simple language with appropriate examples whenever necessary. We expect that the book will solve its purpose and readers will find this book very useful in improving their body language.

Author

CONTENTS

CONTENTS

(1)

Body Language: An Introduction

Body language is a term for communication using body movements or gestures instead of, or in addition to, sounds, verbal language or other communication. It forms part of the category of paralanguage, which describes all forms of human communication that are not verbal language. This includes the most subtle of movements that many people are not aware of, including winking and slight movement of the eyebrows. In addition body language can also incorporate the use of facial expressions.

Studies show that your words account for only 7% of the messages you convey. The remaining 93% is non-verbal. 55% of communication is based on what people see and the other 38% is transmitted through tone of voice. So think about it. In the business setting, people can see what you are not saying. If your body language doesn't match your words, you are wasting your time.

Eye contact is the most obvious way you communicate. When you are looking at the other person, you show interest. When you fail to make eye contact, you give the impression that the other person is of no importance. Maintain eye contact about 60% of the time in order to look interested, but not aggressive.

Facial expression is another form of non-verbal communication. A smile sends a positive message and is appropriate in all but a life and death situation. Smiling adds warmth and an aura of confidence. Others will be more receptive if you remember to check your expression. Your mouth gives clues, too, and not just when you are speaking. Mouth movements, such as pursing your lips or twisting them to one side, can indicate that you are thinking about what you are hearing or that you are holding something back.

The position of your head speaks to people. Keeping your head straight, which is not the same as keeping your head on straight, will make you appear self-assured and authoritative. People will take you seriously. Tilt your head to one side if you want to come across as friendly and open.

Anger-Anger   Fear-Fear

Anger-Fear   Fear-Anger

How receptive you are is suggested by where you place your arms. Arms crossed or folded over your chest say that you have shut other people out and have no interest in them or what they are saying. This position can also say, "I don't agree with you." You might just be cold, but unless you shiver at the same time, the person in front of you may get the wrong message.

How you use your arms can help or hurt your image as well. Waving them about may show enthusiasm to some, but others see this gesture as one of uncertainty and immaturity. The best place for your arms is by your side. You will look confident and relaxed. If this is hard for you, do what you always do when you want to get better at something – practice. After a while, it will feel natural.

The angle of your body gives an indication to others about what's going through your head. Leaning in says, "Tell me more." Leaning away signals you've heard enough. Adding a nod of your head is another way to affirm that you are listening. Posture is just as important as your grandmother always said it was. Sit or stand erect if you want to be seen as alert and enthusiastic. When you slump in your chair or lean on the wall, you look tired. No one wants to do business with someone who has no energy.

Control your hands by paying attention to where they are. In the business world, particularly when you deal with people from other cultures, your hands need to be seen. That would mean you should keep them out of your pockets and you should resist the urge to put them under the table or behind your back. Having your hands anywhere above the neck, fidgeting with your hair or rubbing your face, is unprofessional.

Legs talk, too. A lot of movement indicates nervousness. How and where you cross them tells others how you feel. The preferred positions for the polished professional are feet flat on the floor or legs crossed at the ankles. The least professional and most offensive position is resting one leg or ankle on top of your other knee. Some people call this the "Figure Four." It can make you look arrogant.

The distance you keep from others is crucial if you want to establish good rapport. Standing too close or "in someone's face" will mark you as pushy. Positioning yourself too far away will make you seem standoffish. Neither is what you want so find the happy medium. Most importantly, do what makes the other person feel comfortable. If the person with whom you are speaking keeps backing away from you, stop. Either that person needs space or you need a breath mint. You may not be aware of what you are saying with your body, but others will get the message.

Different types of body language

Body language is an important part of communication which can constitute 50% or more of what we are communicating. If you wish to communicate well, then it makes sense to understand how you can (and cannot) use your body to say what you mean.

Message clusters

Body language comes in clusters of signals and postures, depending on the internal emotions and mental states. Recognising a whole cluster is thus far more reliable than trying to interpret individual elements.

- Aggressive body language: Showing physical threat.
- Attentive body language: Showing real interest.
- Bored body language: Just not being interested.
- Closed body language: Many reasons are closed.
- Deceptive body language: Seeking to cover up lying or other deception.
- Defensive body language: Protecting self from attack.
- Dominant body language: Dominating others.
- Emotional body language: Identifying feelings.
- Evaluating body language: Judging and deciding about something.
- Open body language: Many reasons for being open.
- Power body language: Demonstrating one's power.
- Ready body language: Wanting to act and waiting for the trigger.
- Relaxed body language: Comfortable and unstressed.
- Romantic body language: Showing attraction to others.

- Submissive body language: Showing you are prepared to give in.

Expressions, postures and gestures in some of the above mentioned types of body languages can be simply understood as following.

Aggressive body language

A significant cluster of body movements is used to signal aggression. This is actually quite useful as it is seldom a good idea to get into a fight, even for powerful people.

Fighting can hurt you, even though you are pretty certain you will win. In addition, with adults, fighting is often socially unacceptable and aggression through words and body language is all that may ever happen.

Threat

Facial signals

Much aggression can be shown in the face, from disapproving frowns and pursed lips to sneers and full snarls. The eyes can be used to stare and hold the gaze for long period. They may also squint, preventing the other person seeing where you are looking.

Attack signals

When somebody is about to attack, they give visual signal such as clenching of fists ready to strike and lowering and spreading of the body for stability. They are also likely to give anger signs such as redness of the face.

Exposing oneself

Exposing oneself to attack is also a form of aggression. It is saying 'Go on – I dare you. I will still win.' It can include not looking at the other person, crotch displays, relaxing the body, turning away and so on.

Invasion

Invading the space of the other person in some way is an act of aggression that is equivalent to one country invading another.

False friendship

Invasion is often done under the cloak of familiarity, where you act as if you are being friendly and move into a space reserved for friends, but *without being invited*. This gives the other person a dilemma of whether to repel a 'friendly' advance or to accept dominance of the other.

Approach

When you go inside the comfort zone of others without permission, you are effectively invading their territory. The close you get, the greater your ability to have 'first strike', from which an opponent may not recover.

Touching

Touching the person is another form of invasion. Even touching social touch zones such as arm and back can be aggressive.

Insulting gestures

There are many, many gestures that have the primary intent of insulting the other person and hence inciting them to anger and a perhaps unwise battle. Single and double fingers pointed up, arm thrusts, chin tilts and so on are used, although many of these do vary across cultures (which can make for hazardous accidental movements when you are overseas).

Mock attacks

Gestures may include symbolic action that mimics actual attacks, including waving fingers (the beating baton), shaking fists, head-butts and so on. This is saying 'Here is what I will do to you!'

Physical items may be used as substitutes, for example, banging of tables and doors or throwing . Again, this is saying 'This could be you!'

Large gestures

The size of gestures may also be used to signal levels of aggression, from simple finger movements to whole arm sweeps, sometimes even with exaggerated movements of the entire body.

Attentive Body language

When you are in conversation or otherwise attending to what others are saying or doing, your body sends signals to the other person as to how interested you really are.

Attentive body language sends a strong signal of real and deep interest that is both flattering and likely to result in reciprocal attention.

It was said that if you met with the English 19th century politician William Gladstone, you would come away thinking he was the most intelligent and witty person in the country. If, however, you met his peer Benjamin Disraeli, then you would come away thinking that *you* were the most intelligent and witty person. Disraeli, it would seem, was somewhat more skilled at paying attention.

Listening

A person who is attentive is first of all listening. This can be of varying intensity though attentive listening is deep and interested.

Ignoring distractions

There are many competing stimuli that demand our attention. If a person ignores distraction, from phone calls to other people interrupting, then they send strong and flattering 'I am interested in you' signals.

Stillness

Body movement often betrays distracting thoughts and feelings. When the listener is largely still, the implication is of forgetting everything else except the other person, with not even internal dialogue being allowed to distract.

Leaning forward

When I am interested in you and what you have to say I will likely lean slightly towards you, perhaps better to hear everything you have to say.

Tilted head

An attentive head may be tilted slightly forward. It also may show curiosity when tilted to the side (although this may also indicate uncertainty).

Gaze

An attentive person looks at the other person without taking their gaze away. They will likely blink less, almost for fear of missing something.

Patience

When you want to hear more from the other person you are patient, listening until they have finished speaking and not butting in with your views.

Even when you have something to say or when they pause, you still patiently seek a full understanding of them and give them space in which to complete what they have to say.

Open body

Open body language shows that you are not feeling defensive and are mentally open to what they have to say (and hence not closed to their thoughts).

Slow nodding

Nodding shows agreement and also encourages the other person to keep talking. Fast nodding may show impatience, whilst a slower nod indicates understanding and approval.

Interest noises

Little noises such as 'uh huh' and 'mmm' show that you are interested, understand and want to hear more. They thus encourage the other person to keep talking.

Reflecting

When you reflect the other person back to them they feel affirmed and that you are aligned with them. Reflecting activities range from matching body language to paraphrasing what they say.

Emotional body language

With careful observation, emotions may be detected from non-verbal signs. Remember that these are indicators and not certain guarantees.

Contextual clues may also be used, in particular what is being said to the person or what else is happening around then.

Anger

Anger occurs when achievement of goals are frustrated.

- Neck and/or face is red or flushed.
- Baring of teeth and snarling.

- Clenched fists.
- Leaning forward and invasion of body space.
- Other aggressive body language.
- Use of power body language.

Fear, anxiety and nervousness

Fear occurs when basic needs are threatened. There are many levels of fear, from mild anxiety to blind terror. The many bodily changes caused by fear make it easy to detect.

- A 'cold sweat'.
- Pale face.
- Dry mouth, which may be indicated by licking lips, drinking water, rubbing throat.
- Not looking at the other person.
- Damp eyes.
- Trembling lip.
- Varying speech tone.
- Speech errors.
- Voice tremors.
- Visible high pulse (noticeable on the neck or movement of crossed leg.)
- Sweating.
- Tension in muscles: clenched hands or arms, elbows drawn in to the side, jerky movements, legs wrapped around things.

- Gasping and holding breath.
- Fidgeting.
- Defensive body language, including crossed arms and legs and generally drawing in of limbs.
- Ready body language (for fight-or-flight).
- Other symptoms of stress.

Sadness

Sadness is the opposite of happiness and indicates a depressive state.

- Drooping of the body.
- Trembling lip.
- Flat speech tone.
- Tears.

Embarrassment

Embarrassment may be caused by guilt or transgression of values.

- Neck and/or face is red or flushed.
- Looking down or away from others. Not looking them in the eye.
- Grimacing, false smile, changing the topic or otherwise trying to cover up the embarrassment.

Surprise

Surprise occurs when things occur that were not expected.

- Raised eyebrows.

- Widening of eyes.
- Open mouth.
- Sudden backward movement.

Happiness

Happiness occurs when goals and needs are met.

- General relaxation of muscles.
- Smiling (including eyes).
- Open body language.

How to communicate with body language

It is often said that in face-to-face communications regarding emotions, the words we speak actually account for less than 10% of the message that we convey, while body language accounts for more than half of our message (our tone of voice supposedly communicates the rest).

Body language is important, and if your words say one thing but your body says another, the person you are speaking to is more likely to believe the message your body is communicating. Here's how to start using body language to improve your day-to-day communications and, more importantly, to improve your quality of life.

Some steps

1. Be natural. It's easy to find big lists of what certain gestures mean, and entire dictionaries have been written that attempt to decipher the meaning of every posture, blink of the eye, or muscle twitch. The

meanings of signals differ from one person to the next, however, and there are vast cultural differences, as well. What's more, it is not possible to control all your muscles so that each gesture and facial expression delivers the meaning you want it to deliver. Even if you were to succeed in controlling your body language "by the book," you would look fake.

2. Identify your own body language patterns. People spend a lot of time looking at your body language. What are they seeing?

Make a conscious effort to think about what your body is doing in different interactions with different people. A mirror can be useful to examine facial expressions and posture, but mainly you just want to pay attention to what your body does when you're angry, nervous, happy, etc.

- Determine whether your body language is in sync with your message. Your body language is effective if it communicates the message you want it to communicate. Does your posture communicate confidence, or does it make you seem unsure of yourself even as your words express confidence? If your non-verbal signals match your words, you'll not only communicate more clearly, you'll also be perceived as being more charismatic.

- Look at the big picture. Don't stay awake at night wondering if your right index finger is effectively communicating your approval of something. Different parts of your body work together to communicate meaning in "message clusters," and generally the more strongly you feel about what you're talking about the more parts of the body are actively communicating. You don't have to have every little nuance "correct" as long as the overall effect of the cluster is in sync with your message.

3.   Correct the big problems. If you take away one thing from here, it should be that body language should be natural, and you don't need to obsess over it. That said, there are certain situations that may merit "relearning" certain aspects of your body language.

•   Touching one's face signals anxiety.

    If you give persistent, very obvious counterproductive signals, it may be worth your time to fix them. For example, if you're constantly hunched over or touching your face, you'll never look confident, approachable, or at ease. Improving your posture and working to eliminate nervous tics can be difficult and will take time, but if you focus your efforts only on the big things, you'll quickly improve your overall non-verbal communication.

•   Hand gesture commonly used in Argentina to roughly convey "What the heck are you thinking?"

    If you have recently entered a new culture, you may need to adjust your body language. Cultural norms regarding body language (i.e., how far away you should stand from someone, how much eye contact you should make, and what gestures are considered taboo), vary considerably, and if you don't speak the same body language as the locals, you're liable to be misunderstood a great deal, sometimes with very serious implications.

- Practice in front of a mirror.

  Concentrate on difficult situations. Most of our day-to-day interactions are with people we know fairly well. As people get to know you better, they become better at reading your body language, which means (for better or for worse) that they're less likely to misinterpret your non-verbal cues. With this in mind, then, it's most important to make sure your body language is clear in interactions with people you don't know very well. These situations (first dates or job interviews, for example) may merit some special attention. Get in front of a mirror and practice these interactions. Speak aloud as you normally would, and carefully watch what your body is doing. Even better, videotape yourself for several minutes and then watch the video to identify how you might present yourself better.

4. Have more than one gesture to "get the message across." If you want to make sure you're not misunderstood, repeat both gestures when you speak the idea aloud. If the listener doesn't pick up on one gesture, he or she will likely be familiar with the other. You don't have to use a body language gesture (or two) for every word, but it's a good idea to have

a toolbox of gestures you can use to reinforce very important, but easily misinterpreted, concepts.

5. Direct the most positive gestures toward the listener. This way you more clearly indicate that you are offering a favourable outcome to the listener as though it were a gift to them. Direct the most negative gestures away from yourself and the listener. This way you clearly indicate that you wish that no obstacle stands in the way of your intended message.

6. Say what you mean. For most people, appropriate body language—that is, body language that effectively reinforces the speaker's meaning—comes naturally when they mean what they say. The problem, of course, is that we don't always say what we mean. If you're trying to lie convincingly, for example, you'll probably have to alter your body language to prevent it from arousing suspicion. Even when we're not trying to deceive we may not really be saying what we feel. If your boyfriend or girlfriend asks if you love him or her, you may think you do but also think you don't; the mixed feelings may come out in a mixed message, in which your words say "yes," but your body language portrays your doubt. While much is said about changing your body language to communicate what you want to say, it's often easier to just say what you feel.

7. Use your body language to help you understand how you feel. If you're not quite sure how you feel about something or someone, pay attention to what your

body is saying. Just as other people can read your body language to help uncover what you're feeling, you can learn from your body, and, for the most part, you should be able to read your body language better than anyone else can—all you have to do is pay attention. Using body language effectively means not only communicating with others, but also learning more about yourself.

8. Treat the cause, not the symptoms. Body language is very useful as a self-improvement tool, because it can clue us into our own feelings: our strengths, our fears, our hopes, our instincts. There's a multi-million dollar industry filled with people who will tell you how to position your torso and move your eyes in order to look more confident around members of the opposite sex or to seem more competent at work, but the usefulness of such instruction is limited. Even with dedicated practice, body language is hard to convincingly fake. Even if you manage to use your non-verbal cues to communicate feelings you don't really feel, you may, in the end, discover that you are only fooling yourself.

9. Pay attention to your emotions and keep from becoming overwhelmed. Emotion is often one of the primary factors that people use to drive themseleves to choose specific gestures for their method of communication. Certain situations may call for stressed forms of body usages, however for most purposes it is probably more beneficial to remain

calm. If you are calm, you are less likely to say and do things you'll later regret, things that could be destructive to your communication efforts. If you are calm you are more likely to be free and open, rather than withdrawn or defensive.

How to read body language

Understanding body language is a skill that can enhance your life. You can know what a person thinks and feels by examining their subconscious body language.

Some steps in reading body language

1. Gauge the distance. The closer that someone is to you, the warmer his or her opinions are of you. The farther away that someone is, the less they care.

2. Watch their head position.

    • Overly tilted heads are a potential sign of sympathy. Alternatively the person is trying to convince you of their honesty.

    • Lowered heads indicate a reason to hide something. Take note if someone lowers their head. If it is when he or she are complimented, he or she may be shy, ashamed, timid, keeping distance from the other person, in disbelief, or thinking to herself. If it is after an explanation, then he or she may be unsure if what they said was correct.

3. Look into their eyes.

    • Liars will consecutively look at you and look away a number of times. You can actually learn specifically how to observe behaviour to judge whether someone's lying.

- People who look away while supposedly listening to you are thinking about something else. This is why when you are talking to a group of people, if an item in conversation strikes the one looking away, they will ask for you to repeat the story.

- Auditory learners may look from side-to-side and repeat phrases in an effort to retain information.

4. See if they're mirroring you. Mirroring is another common gesture. If someone mirrors, or mimics your appearance, this is a very genuine sign that they are interested in you.

5. Check their arms.

- People with crossed arms are closing themselves to social influence. The worst thing that you can do to people with crossed arms is to challenge them in one way or another, no matter how they react. This annoys them. Though some people just cross their arms as a habit, they're (slightly) reserved, or they're just trying to hide something on their shirt.

- If someone rests their arms behind their neck, they are open to what is being discussed and interested in listening more. They may be waiting to state their opinion on the matter.

- Look at the location of their hands. If their hands are in their pockets, then they are more relaxed and are more likely to be attracted to you. For example, when a man has his hands in his pockets, with his thumbs outside, pointing down, then he is trying to draw your attention down there. This can also be transferred to other parts of the body and objects.

6.   Be aware of nervous gestures.

- If someone brushes their hair back with their fingers, their thoughts about something conflict with yours. They might not voice this. If you see raised eyebrows during this time, you can be pretty sure that they disagree with you.

- If someone is biting their lip, they are anticipating something.

- Lowered eyebrows and squinted eyes illustrate an attempt at understanding what is being said or going on. It's usually skeptical. (Or maybe they have a problem seeing)

Understand body language

There are various estimates on how much of our communication is verbal and how much is non-verbal. In any case, body language is very important in all aspects of our lives to getting your true message across and interpreting the message of others.

Here is a beginner's guide. These are very general, and in many cases, do not apply. Posture is often affected by physical issues, fatigue, an injury etc.

Important steps

1. Looking

- When you look strangers in the eye, you are saying, "I want to know more about you."

- When you look people in the mouth, you are saying, "I am not comfortable looking into your eyes."

- When your eyes are locked onto a specific part of a person's face you are saying, "I am nervous."

- When you look away from a person routinely or lean away from them, you are saying, "I don't like you."

- When you raise one eyebrow, you are saying, "oh really?"

- When you look upwards, you are saying, "I am thinking."

- When you close your eyes halfway, you are saying, "I am suspicious."

- When you widen your eyes, you are saying, "I am amazed."

2. Expressing yourself through facial features.

- When you wink you are saying, "It's our little secret."

- When you smile subtly, you are saying, "Here is a gesture of approval."

- When you smile with teeth and close your eyes a bit, you are saying, "I am very happy."

- When you frown, you are saying, "I am bored/ unhappy."

- When you drop your jaw, you are saying, "I don't believe it."

- When you bite your bottom lip, you are saying, "I'm flirty."

3. Moving your head.

- When your head is up, you are saying, "I don't mind people looking at me."

- When your head is down, you are saying, "I don't want people to look at me."

- When you turn your head to look at someone, you are saying, "I enjoy looking at you."

4. Placing your legs.

- When you hold your legs close together, you are saying, "I am modest."

- When you hold your legs far apart, you are saying, "I am not modest."

5. Placing your shoulders.

- When your shoulders are open and wide, you are saying, "I would like to meet new people."

- When your shoulders are closed and hunched, you are saying, "Leave me alone, please."

6. Contacting physically.

- When you touch someone on the arm, you are saying, "I want us to be close."

- When you touch someone on the waist/neck/face, you are saying, "I am physically attracted to you."

7. Understanding the general condition.

- When you are tense, you are saying, "I am not comfortable."

- When you are relaxed, you are saying, "I am comfortable."

- When you fidget, you are saying, "I want to find something better to do."

2

Nonverbal Behaviour and Communication

Nonverbal communication has been referred to as "body language" in popular culture ever since the publication of Julius Fast's book of the same name in 1970.

However, researchers Mark Knapp and Judith Hall have defined nonverbal communication as follows: "Nonverbal communication refers to communication effected by means other than words." This definition does not exclude many forms of communication, but it implies that nonverbal communication is more than body language. However, determination of the exact boundaries of the field is a point of contention among scholars.

Nonverbal communication is an area of study that straddles many disciplines—sociology, psychology, anthropology, communication, and even art and criminal justice. Each of these fields tends to focus on a slightly different aspect of nonverbal communication. For example, psychology might focus on the nonverbal expression of emotions; anthropology might focus on the use of interpersonal space in different cultures; and communication might focus on the content of the message. However, there is more overlap among these fields than divergence.

It appears that all cultures have written or oral traditions expressing the importance of nonverbal communication to understanding human beings. Over thousands of years, Chinese culture has developed a set of rules about how to judge the character and personality of an individual by observing the size, shape, and relative positions of the nose, eyes, eyebrows, chin, cheeks, and forehead. Someone with wide-set eyes would be a "broadminded" person, while someone with a high forehead would be a "smart" person. Although there does not seem to be much scientific evidence that facial characteristics predict personality, modern people still believe this to be valid.

Ancient Greek culture has also relied on non-verbal communication to understand people. The playwright Theophrastus created a list of "31 types of men" that he made available to other playwrights to assist them in the creation of characters for their plays. Theophrastus relied on insights gleaned from nonverbal communication to describe these personalities; the penurious man does not wear his sandals until noon, and the sanguine man has slumped shoulders. Humans still rely on nonverbal insights like these to judge the personalities and emotions of other people.

In India, the sacred Hindu texts called the *Veda*, written around 1000 B.C.E., described a liar as someone who, when questioned, rubs his big toe along the ground, looks down, does not make eye contact, and so forth. Late-twentieth-century research based on North Americans shows that people still concur with the *Veda* on this description of a liar.

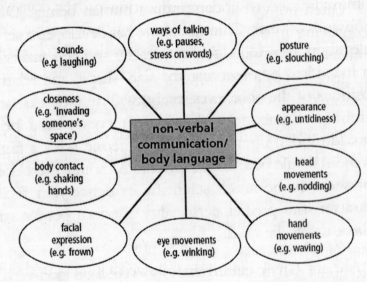

It is important to note that how we make ourselves known through, for example, a look, gesture, postural shift or trembling voice. At the very outset, however, it should be stressed that distinguishing between verbal and nonverbal communication is not as conceptually straightforward as it might at first seem. Neither are the two operationally discrete. For the most part in our everyday social contact verbal and nonverbal codes are complexly intertwined, each to varying degrees defining the other in the overall process of carrying meaning.

The look on our faces as words are uttered, the glint in our eyes, dismissive gestures of the hand, the tension in our bodies, and such like, will most probably be overlooked. It is unlikely though that our listeners neglect these nonverbal nuances.

Often nonverbal communication proves decisive in conveying information and making judgements about others. Relating successfully to others demands the ability to display appropriate nonverbal behaviour but also to be sensitive to the nonverbal messages of others.

Fascination with nonverbal aspects of social intercourse can be traced back at least to Aristotle. In the teaching of rhetoric in classical and medieval times, forms of specific gesture were identified along with their planned effects on an audience. It is only relatively recently though that social scientists have devoted much concerted attention to nonverbal matters. This followed a long period during which the topic was depreciated, being regarded as inconsequential, and those interested in it as academically suspect.

For example, someone described nonverbal education as a subject which is, 'for academic and ecclesiastical purposes, non-existent and may be safely ignored altogether or left, with a patronising smile, to those whom the Pharisees of verbal orthodoxy call cranks, quacks, charlatans and unqualified amateurs'. Such milestones in the evolution of the subject as Charles Darwin's The expression of emotion in man and animals only began to receive serious social scientific recognition in the last few decades. During this time, though, growth of interest has burgeoned leading to significant theoretical, conceptual and empirical advances in the field as witnessed by countless publications of books, book chapters and articles. There is even a well-established journal, the Journal of Nonverbal Behavior, now devoted to disseminating major work in this area. What was once described by someone as the 'foundling child of the social sciences-disdained, neglected, even nameless', has found its place as a respected member of the family.

Indeed the multi-faceted study of non verbal communication now draws inspiration from disciplines beyond the established boundaries of social science. As well as contributions from social psychology, anthropology, sociology and psychiatry, perspectives are being offered from, for instance, ethology and neurophysiology. Here is a rich seam being worked by what traditionally has been in many ways two quite distinct types of miner, the social and the natural scientist, each with different sets of tools used to exploit individually appraised pay-dirt. In non verbal communication it seems that both have found a common area of fascination and are beginning to become aware of and appreciate the contributions of the other.

Some believe that non verbal communication is currently one of the foremost sites of a rapprochement between biology and social science as respective researchers investigate such fundamental issues as the extent to which nonverbal behaviour is culturally prescribed or naturally determined.

Locating nonverbal communication

Although the division between verbal and nonverbal communication defies any sharp delineation, non verbal communication can be thought of broadly as all forms of direct communication not exclusively relying on the use of words, written or spoken.

Some consideration has already been given to definitional issues surrounding communication in general, and will not be repeated. Rather we will focus here on the 'nonverbal' rather than the 'communication' element of non verbal communication. At first sight, crafting a sharp definition of 'nonverbal' might seem like an easier task, but even here things are less than straightforward.

In a piece of early but still influential work, Laver and Hutcheson distinguished between verbal and nonverbal, and vocal and non-vocal communication. Vocal behaviour refers to all aspects of speech including language content and accompanying expressions such as tone of voice, rate of speech and accent, etc. Non-vocal behaviour, in contrast, refers to all other bodily activities that have a communicative function such as facial expressions, gestures and movements. These are sometimes referred to as body language. Verbal behaviour, on the other hand, is taken to mean the actual words and language used while nonverbal behaviour refers to all vocal and non-vocal behaviour that is not verbal.

This system seems therefore to insert a sharp and clearly recognisable dividing line between the verbal and the nonverbal, until it is realised that verbal communication has a non-vocal element. It encompasses types of gestural communication such as formal sign language that one may have expected to find listed as nonverbal. According to Richmond precise definitions that introduce hard and fast distinctions between verbal and nonverbal communication are illusory. Instead they suggested teasing the two forms apart by pointing up broad differences. As such, by comparison, verbal messages:

- rely much more heavily on symbols (i.e. words) as part of an arbitrary code;
- tend to be discretely packaged in separate words rather than represented in continuous behaviour, as in gaze;
- carry more meaning explicitly rather than implicitly;
- typically address cognitive/propositional rather than emotional/relational matters.

Someone further noted that verbal interchanges must take place sequentially (i.e. participants must take turns) but interactors can communicate simultaneously using a nonverbal code.

Here we concentrate on communication by, for instance, tone of voice, talk speed, volume of speech and intonation. In addition to these nonverbal aspects of speech, information is transmitted and received through a whole range of body movements such as the posture adopted when sitting in a chair-is it stiff, upright and symmetrical suggesting tension or anxiety or is the person sprawled down in the chair suggesting a feeling of relaxation or familiarity? Faces, too, play an important role in social encounters by at times giving some expression to our inner thoughts, such as showing delight when presented with an unexpected gift or displaying sadness when told about the death of a close friend. A smile can also suggest approachability and availability for friendly relational contact.

Before we open our mouths to speak our physical appearance conveys a great deal of information about our age, sex, occupation, status (if a certain uniform is worn) and personality. For someone with the unnerving perceptual acuity of a Sherlock Holmes in matters of social observation, such cues may become the veritable words of biography.

In Arthur Conan Doyle placed the following words in the mouth of the great sleuth: By a man's finger-nails, by his coat-sleeve, by his boot, by his trouser-knees, by the callosities of his forefinger and thumb, by his expression, by his shirt-cuffs-by each of these things a man's calling is plainly revealed.

As a manifestation of physical attraction, the powerful effects of appearance on favourable judgements of such attributes as intelligence, warmth, friendliness and social confidence are well documented.

Not only are we concerned with the appearance and behaviour of the person involved in communication but, in addition, environmental factors such as architecture, furniture, decoration, smells, colour, texture and noise can reflect on the person inhabiting that space and shape interpersonal contact. These examples give some idea of the categories to which nonverbal behaviour attends.

The importance of nonverbal communication

Talk of non verbal communication, especially in the context of improving social relations, typically provokes one of two contrasting and equally extreme reactions. Some, the 'disciples', prepare themselves for a quasi-mystical experience during which will be revealed the great lexicon by means of which all man's (including woman's) deepest (and often darkest) secrets can be deciphered. In the diametrically opposed camp are the 'cynics' who tend to hold the line that all such talk is at best both pretty obvious to anyone with a modicum of social intelligence and decidedly over-rated; at worst, it is so much 'hocus pocus'. Reality unquestionably lies somewhere between these poles.

While non verbal communication should not be regarded as the holy grail of interpersonal involvement, neither can it be dismissed as a wholly discredited relic. One of the earliest authorities in the field, persuasively argued the importance of appreciating the key role of nonverbal processes in communication. He claimed that the average person actually speaks for a total of only ten to eleven minutes daily; the standard spoken sentence taking only about 2.5 seconds. There can be little prospect of successful face-to-face interaction in situations where interactors have little appreciation of their own non verbal communication or sensitivity to that of the other.

This is equally true in everyday situations and in those of professional practice. The role of non verbal communication has been acknowledged for instance in management, education, nursing, law and medicine. In the latter study, the research team was able to predict the academic grades assigned to medical students by their clinical supervisors by rating a sample of students' nonverbal behaviour while interacting with patients in a paediatric setting. Riggio proposed that being nonverbally skilful involved an expressive element, an element of sensitivity, and one of control over performance.

Purposes of nonverbal communication

Just why we should make use of non verbal communication is a very legitimate question. We are the only species with this marvellously abstract and sophisticated means of communicating that we call language. Other species display various forms of nonverbal behaviour. Through changes in, for example, real or apparent size, posture and movement, odour and skin colour, and with a myriad of grunts, screams and roars, they convey information about bodily and emotional states, social status and territorial ownership. But language is different. It frees us from the here and now, from the physical and actual. Without it we would find it difficult or impossible to refer to, never mind take into account, abstract concepts such as love, loyalty or honour; happenings at this point in time in another place; happenings in the past; happenings in the future; things that have never happened and probably never will (including the whole literary genre of fiction).

The remainder of the matter will be devoted to a brief mapping of different forms that nonverbal behaviour can take. Before doing so, however, we will extend some of the points by taking a look at the uses to which non verbal communication is put.

Replacing verbal communication

Some non verbal communication, especially in the form of gestures, is used as a direct substitute for words in circumstances where speech is either not feasible or not desirable. It may be that interactors have neither hearing nor speech, relying entirely on the use of hand, arm or mouth movements as part of recognised signing systems allowing communication to take place. Sometimes, on the other hand, individuals are temporarily denied a suitable channel to facilitate speech, and so resort to some form of gesture-based contact.

This is particularly evident among deep-sea divers, for instance, when working under water. In other situations, excessive ambient noise may make talking impossible.

Alternatively, interactors may find themselves too far apart to have a normal conversation necessitating some alternative such as semaphore or the tick-tack system of signalling used by racecourse bookmakers. Secrecy may be a further reason for not wishing to talk publicly. In different sports, team members can be seen using nonverbal cues to call the proposed play at different stages of the game.

Complementing the spoken word

Nonverbal behaviour is often used alongside what is said in a way that is consistent with it. In so doing, the verbal message may be clarified, extended or enhanced. In an analysis of college lecturers' deliveries, two researchers found that bursts of figurative language and spontaneous pictorial gestures tended to occur at points where the lecturer dealt with material beyond the students' normal experience or offered a different interpretation of a familiar topic. When both modes overlapped, gestures served to augment the metaphoric.

Some material, such as giving elaborate directions, or describing an irregular shape, can be difficult to get across in words alone. In order to facilitate the overall message an imaginary map or outline is sometimes drawn in the air while describing the route or object. Someone referred to these gestural acts as illustrators and they will be examined later when discussing gestures. By observing people in conversations it can be noted that these accompanying movements actually facilitate speech where it is difficult to describe aspects of space and shape in purely verbal terms. They may also assist in the tasks of learning and remembering. In research carried out by a researcher, participants watched video recordings of children speaking and gesturing about the concept featured in the conversation and were then tested for immediate recognition of information carried verbally and by gesture. Nine- and ten-year-old children, tested in this way, performed poorly in processing contradictory messages resulting from a mismatch between the verbal and gestural. Interestingly, 7-8 year olds and college students were more successful. A significant age effect was also reported, but the complexity of the verbal message played a part as well. They discovered that accompanying gestures that complemented instructions aided comprehension for pre-school children but not those in kindergarten. Likewise gestures at odds with the verbal information were detrimental for kindergarten but not pre-school children. This effect disappeared, though, when the verbal message was simplified.

Nonverbal cues can also complement language in other ways involving propositional and emotional messages. Sympathising with someone is done much more convincingly when the sympathiser's overall demeanour mirrors what is said.

Purposes of nonverbal communication

Non verbal communication is used to:

1 *Replace verbal* communication in situations where it may be impossible or inappropriate to talk.

2 *Complement verbal* communication, thereby enhancing the overall message.

3 *Modify the spoken word.*

4 *Contradict,* either intentionally or unintentionally, what is said.

5 *Regulate conversation* by helping to mark speech turns.

6 *Express emotions and interpersonal attitudes.*

7 *Negotiate relationships* in respect of, for instance, dominance, control and liking.

8 *Convey personal and social identity* through such features as dress and adornments.

9 *Contextualise interaction* by creating a particular social setting.

Types of nonverbal communication

Non verbal communication can take the following forms:

Haptics–communication through physical touch.

Kinesics–communication through body movement (e.g. gestures, head nods, posture, eye-contact, facial expression).

Proxemics-messages conveyed through the perception and

use of personal and social space (e.g. interpersonal distance, territoriality).

Physical characteristics-information revealed through body shape, size and adornments.

Environmental factors-messages carried by features of the social surroundings such as furniture, decor and lighting.

Vocalics–communication by means of the nonverbal elements of speech (e.g. voice pitch, resonance, and so on).

3

The Role of Body Movements in Communication

When we think of body movements as communicative events, most of us are likely to get rather dramatic in our fantasies. A phrase that comes readily to mind is "body language," and there has even been a book from the popular press with that phrase as its title. The topic has everything: the hope of reading the romantic intentions of one's girl- or boyfriend, the adventure of outsmarting a shrewd salesman, the sure thing of predicting the next move of a poker-faced gambler, the surprise of "reading through" the white lies of one's friends, the advantage of knowing what a prospective employer wants to hear.

Everybody knows, of course, that these fantasies are fantasies, that nobody can make himself invisible and listen in on forbidden conversations. And yet there is a lot of truth in the notion that people communicate in many different ways, by words, by tone of voice, by facial expressions, by body movements, by the use of the physical space between one person and another, even by certain psychophysiological responses like blushing and speed or depth of breathing. We are constantly reading each other, or trying to, using all the information we can get, and we can get it from a lot more sources than just the words that pass between us. The question here is whether all these sources of information can properly be called language, and what difference it might make if they could or could not be. There are many other communication media, such as facial expressions, and the principles by which this analysis is organized are general ones and could be applied to those behaviors as well.

The first thing to do in deciding whether any given set of behaviors is a language is to agree on what a language is. That will be the first task here, spelling out some useful criteria for categorising body movements as either language or not language. It turns out that there is no handy sharp dividing line for this dichotomy, but there are still some good guidelines, and there won't be much difficulty in applying them.

Next, two genuine languages that use body movements will be described in terms of these guidelines. One is in common use today: the sign language of the deaf. There are many remaining unknowns about this language, but the version of it used in some western countries, is currently under study by a number of linguists, and there are many "native speakers" of it available when examples are needed.

Body Language: Is it a Code?

From languages using body movements as their medium to "body language" as that term is used so often today, is a long step. When we talk about body language, we do not mean that we really carry on conversations through our bodies about any and all topics, but rather that there is more to conversation than an audio tape or a typescript of the words could tell us. We mean that people express themselves in all sorts of ways, sometimes adding to, sometimes- and this is the interesting part—altering or negating what they are saying in words. When we say we are "really reading" someone, we mean that we are tuned in on all of these wavelengths. Sometimes that is good, when we are feeling really at home with a friend, and sometimes it makes us uncomfortable, when the messages we feel we are getting do not add up to a very friendly total atmosphere.

But how dependable are these messages, in the sense that language is a dependable method of communicating? To answer it, the best set of concepts is that of coding: to the extent that the source information for any system of communication is coded and the elements that make up the messages are also coded, the result is precise communication. Conversely, to the extent that the material has not been subjected to the coding processes, we are left guessing about what the messages really are. To anticipate briefly, there are a few body movements that behave like coded material in that they are easily understood by all or most members of the community. By far the greater majority of movements, however, serve more as cues from which we make inferences. If all the cues add up right, our guesses from these messages can be very good ones, but usually we don't have time for much inferring if we are to keep up with the conversation, and besides, because of the way our perceptual apparatus works, our attention in conversations is drawn to decoding the speech.

First a word about a couple of other interlocking issues. Usually when we talk about "communication" we are referring to situations where one person is deliberately sending messages to one another. He *intends* to do so, and his intentions are fully conscious. Those two characteristics, in fact, are part and parcel of many writers' definitions of communication. But the very idea of body language as it is usually thought of, especially when it refers to cues from which we infer something about a person, precludes both awareness and intention as necessary features of the process. Indeed, some of the stuff that these messages are made of, such as fidgetiness or generalised muscular tension, could not be controlled even if we intended to do so. Others, like posture and how often we look at our conversational partner, are so automatic as to be out of our usual range of consciously thought-out activities. Therefore, the term "communication" will have to take on a more general sort of meaning. It should not be dropped as a term, however, because the messages in question are still messages whether they are deliberate ones or not: they still consist of information of some sort that is transmitted from one person to another. Both the deliberate messages and not-so-deliberate ones should obey the same laws and be accounted for by the same concepts and theories. So communication is still a good word to cover *all* messages that pass between us.

In order to examine the various movements that comprise body language from the standpoint of coding, one of the basic concepts introduced earlier needs to be spelled out more precisely: the one of categorical information. It came up first in connection with the simplifying and regularising process we use in boiling our thought down into concepts. Information that has been treated this way is called discrete information. It comes in separate, distinct packages that do not overlap each other, and these are usually of a finite, countable number.

This sort of information has another characteristic, too: the packages recur again and again, and are made up of roughly the same elements in the same configuration each time they reappear. In short, they become categories to which some community of people may assign labels or meanings. In the case of simplifying thought processes for use in language, we form our thoughts, ideas, and impressions into categories to be used over and over again, and the language community agrees to stick to those categories or concepts as their medium of exchange, and name them with words or signs.

The opposite of discrete information is the continuous, in which there may be an infinite number of values distributed along a continuum, each one shading into the next one imperceptably. One of the features of continuous information is that it can be made artifically discrete by dividing the continuum into step intervals as we do every day in stating our age. No adult ever gives his age in steps any finer than the year unless he is specially asked to, and we have much broader age categories where we do not require the precision that years can give: baby, child, teenager, young adult, and so on. Everyone knows, of course, that these categories are artificially imposed on what is really a continuum, that not all eight-year-olds are the same age. We know, too, that the apparent nonoverlapping character of the age categories is illusory, that some pairs of eight-year-olds are more different in age than some pairs made up of an eight-year-old and a nine-year-old. But for most practical purposes a finer distinction is not needed: we know roughly what is meant by "an eight-year-old child."

In dealing with body movements there is another use of the two terms, discrete and continuous, and that is how movements appear in time. Some are performed discretely-the head nod is a good example—that is, they are brief movements that begin and end suddenly and are sharply separated from the movements that precede them and also from those that follow. Other movements are continuous over time-like one hand stroking the other— and are not seen as different events in time but rather as an activity that spans some period of time.

This difference between discretely performed and continuous movements has two features that are important to understand in the discussion that follows: First, continuous movements cannot sensibly be made into discrete categories simply by dividing them into step intervals. We might divide them, all right, at the changes in direction of continuous stroking, for example, but there would be no meaningful way of naming the resulting categories. On the contrary, we may more easily transform discretely performed movements into continuous information, both as we notice them in social situations and also as we study them in the laboratory, by counting their frequency of occurrence over some period of time. We may then use the results of our counting to make such statements as, "Sachin nods more frequently when talking to Deepika than he does when talking to Rajat."

The second thing to note about the use of continuous and discrete in talking about movements is that not all discrete movements are necessarily categories of movement. The head nod is both: it is performed discretely, and it is recognised as a category of movement whose meaning is agreed upon by members of the language community. In answer to a question that calls for a "Yes" or a "No," a nod means "Yes." In conversations, listeners insert nods from time to time, and while their meaning is not quite so specific, they are still very wordlike, interchangeable with "M-hm," "I see," and so on. Thus the head nod is both discrete and categorical. Many other discretely performed movements, however, do not make up categories that any group might agree has any meaning. Some of the gesticulations that accompany talking, such as those that seem to punctuate the rhythm of speech, are a good case in point. They are usually performed discretely in time, have distinct beginnings and endings, but most of them do not fall into nameable categories. They can be counted, as nods can, and their frequency used as continuous information, and this is the most common way these movements have been dealt with in research studies.

The elements of body language

In describing ASL (American Sign Language) and ISL (Indian Sign Language), it was possible to enumerate all the elemental movements, positions, and configurations of the hands that make up the larger groupings called signs. The elements, and the larger groupings as well, are discrete and categorical in nature, agreed upon by the language community. In body language it is not clear that there exists any set number of elements of this sort: perhaps some movements or postures could be thought of as proper elements, while others could not. This discussion will leave the question open at the outset by listing those behaviors that have been studied by various researchers, and treating them as candidates for elemental categories. No claim for completeness is made, because of the practical considerations researchers must weigh in deciding what to study: they want to study what they think is important according to the theoretical ideas they hold, but they also want some assurance of success, and they may be tempted to stick to things that will be easier to handle with the techniques they already have available. Most investigators also include items that others have studied, partly because there may be alternative theories that may thus be put to the test, and partly as a check on their methods. The most likely candidates for elements in a body language system will be listed here first, the discrete, categorical behaviors, then some that are less likely, and so on down the line.

Categorical Behaviours

Emblems are the most eligible of the discrete, categorical behaviours. They are the movements that have meaning and may be translated directly into words. In some parts of the world, such as Mediterranean countries, a quite complete system of emblems has been worked out and has been used for centuries by people who can hear perfectly well. Some of the stories of these gesture languages may have been exaggerated by the astonished (and artistically gifted) visitors who have described them, but clearly those people's gesture vocabulary enables them to carry on conversations far beyond the bounds that American speakers of English can do with anything but words. Mallery quotes Alexandre Dumas recounting two narratives he observed in Sicily and southern Italy, where he had an opportunity to check independently on what the Italian translation was. Efron describes emblems used by southern Italian immigrants to New York City, and the republication of his work includes a short dictionary of these gestures.

We are not entirely lacking in emblems but their number is probably not large. Many are highly pantomimic so that it would be difficult to decide if they are truly symbolic emblems—if indeed anyone had already decided that only the symbolic could qualify as emblems. The hitch-hiker's movement for thumbing a ride, for example, when it is used in its usual context, does not require an interpreter of some strange language to translate. Circling the ear with the index finger to say, "He's crazy!". Just how many emblems we have is not known precisely, although a survey is currently being made, nor is there any information on how frequently they are used in comparison to other movements day by day. A number of facial expressions other than those of emotion are emblems, and the emotional expressions themselves, may be used as emblems—the surprise expression, for example, to refer to an experience of surprise. Whether the actual facial expressions of emotion are emblems is a moot point since they seem to be biologically determined. Certainly they function as emblems in daily life.

A related sort of movement, probably used more commonly, is referred to by Birdwhistell as the *kinesic marker.* These movements mark some aspect of the speech that is going on at the same time, such as head movements to indicate the person in a group to whom the speaker is referring in some part of his utterance (similar to ASL (American Sign Language) but not so precisely defined). Other such markers may serve as place holders in presenting contrasting ideas, to accompany "On the one hand ... while on the other ...," and the like.

Eye contact may seem an odd behaviour to include in a chapter on body movement, but one of the best ways of identifying it in a research situation is by observing the accompanying head movements: one usually turns his head to look at another person (if the two are not squared off to begin with, and people in our culture seldom place themselves that way), and if one is looking at another, he is usually looking in his eyes. Since people do not maintain eye contact for long periods at a time, the beginning and end of each contact can easily be told, and the behavior qualifies as discrete. Since it is repeated the same way each time, it is a categorical behaviour.

The *smile* is an unmistakable facial behavior that has a sudden onset and usually a slow fade, and is usually of short enough duration to be called a discrete event. Smiles are not all the same, and there may be some subcategories that could be identified, although this work has only begun. One possible subtype is the listener smile, which has both sudden onset and sudden fade and appears to be another equivalent to the head nod and brief vocalisation ("m-hm," etc.).

The *nod* is a discrete, categorical behaviour whose dual meanings ("yes" and "m-hm") were mentioned earlier. There may be other categories of nod, based perhaps on number of movements, but these, along with other smiles, have not been studied sufficiently for any definite statements at this time.

These three discrete, categorical behaviors, eye contact, smiles, and nods, lend themselves to forming continuous variables by counting their frequencies over longer periods of time. Most research studies concentrate on these frequencies, and people in social situations probably do, too: one notices that a friend is smiling a lot more today than last week, or a lot less, and so on. In addition, eye contact can be treated as a continuous variable by measuring the duration of each contact, or by totalling the duration of contact in a larger time period.

The *head shake,* meaning "no," usually occurs only in answer to questions that demand either a "yes" or a "no," and since those questions are rather rare, so is the head shake. The movement may also be seen in an almost continuous form in some people under some circumstances, such as during the expression (in words) of a strongly positive attitude: a person may say, "There was really beautiful photography in that movie," while shaking his head continuously.

Two postures that are discrete and categorical round out this part of the list: *arms akimbo* (or hands on hips) and the *open-closed positions of arms or legs* (hands and arms apart and knees separated for open, and arms crossed or folded and legs crossed for closed). There is some question about whether these should be called elements in the same sense, since there are many ways of striking these poses, but the variations are not great, and they do fall into definite categories. The akimbo posture is probably rare except in the standing position.

Possibly discrete and categorical behaviours

These are all variations of posture and position, and the variables on which they are measured are certainly continuous. Yet it appears that the continua are divided into step intervals just as age was seen to be, in the explanation of discrete and continuous information. The result is a set of categories within each of the behaviours.

Forward and backward lean may be measured in degrees

of the trunk from the vertical, a measurement that is obviously on a continuum. But as we interact with people, we cannot discriminate between slight differences in number of degrees, and we do not need to for the most practical purposes. We need only to be able to say that a person is sitting upright, is leaning forward or leaning backward.

We may go further than that in some cases, saying that he is leaning slightly forward, way forward, and so on, but these are still discrete steps made of an underlying continuum. The fact that they are so easy to name indicates that they are treated as categories.

Distance between persons is also clearly a continuum, but it, too, is commonly divided into discrete step intervals, again perhaps only three: too close, comfortable distance, and too far. Just where the dividing lines are between these intervals depends on the sex and age composition of the group of people involved, and on the culture they come from.

Body orientation means the angle formed by imaginary lines drawn through the shoulders of two people interacting. If they are facing each other squarely the angle is 0°. The usual conversational angle is a little less than 90°. It is not so clear for this variable, that discrete steps are made by people in ordinary, day-to-day situations, but it may work something like distance in that very low angles are too close and at some point beyond the right angle it becomes too distant.

Continuous behaviours

These are intrinsically continuous over time, not discrete movements made into continuous variables by counting how often they occur. *Adaptors* are often intrinsically continuous movements, such as stroking an arm or a leg, playing with a pencil, rubbing one hand with the other, squeezing the fingers of one hand in the other, moving the hands back and forth over the arm of a chair. While these movements, like all others, have beginnings and endings, we tend not to notice those features, and in research many such movements seem most meaningfully measured in terms of their duration. Some take on the appearance of fidgetiness, but just now people in social situations notice them-or if they do at all-is not known.

Rhythmical movements of various parts of the body are also performed continuously. They include foot swinging (usually with legs crossed), foot tapping, finger drumming, and a number of others.

There are a number of other continuous movements that have not been studied specifically, but which may be noticeable in social situations. Certain movements of the feet comprise one group, flexing, turning, and the like; sometimes these movements are almost invisible because the person is moving his toes inside his shoes. Turning back and forth in a swivel chair or rocking in a rocker, when those chairs are present, make up another group.

The organisation of body language

In the description of languages so far, organisation has been an easy topic, because the elements of those languages are arranged very systematically into the groupings that make up their words and signs, with relatively little variation permitted in the total configuration for each. Emblems probably behave in about the same way, although they have not been studied enough for anyone to say for sure. Neither do we know whether they occur frequently enough to be considered an important part of body language in the usual sense of that term. Other than emblems, there appear to be only a few groupings to talk about. Chief among these are postures: in the arms akimbo and the open-closed positions, a total of elements adds up to what the viewer interprets as one of those positions. But the way the elements are arranged is quite variable. In arms akimbo position, the hands may be open or made into a fist, the hands may be rotated forward or backward, and they may be placed toward the front or the back just so long as they are vaguely on the hips, and so on. For any of these variations, a number of viewers would agree that the person is standing "with arms akimbo." The open—closed positions can be made up of even more variable elements.

Some of the acts under discrete, categorical behaviours might be considered groupings, since they contain more than one movement—the head nod, for example-but those constituents are so few that to talk about organisation into a larger grouping seems like over-formalising things. This is not to say that there may not be more than one kind of nod, depending on the details of the constituent movements, but we need a good deal more research on these details before we can differentiate among such acts in a useful way.

Most of the organisation of body movements we ordinarily think of as making up body language is determined by the organisation of the concurrent speech. As we talk, we divide up our stream of talk into packages of a few words, and these are marked by rhythmical features like recurring stresses toward the end of each unit and a characteristic slowing down as the unit is finished. The organisation of these units is made up of the syntactic rules, or grammar, of the language. Many body movements follow this unit formation, as if the fact of speaking were a powerful determiner of much of what the speaker does at the same time. When the speaker looks at his listener, and how he changes his line of regard (and also the direction his head is facing); when he inserts the kinesic markers to indicate who is being referred to, to emphasise one topic or another, or whatever; when he initiates the more random–appearing gesticulations–all these are tied to the rhythm structure of the speech that the movements are accompanying. Even larger movements such as posture shifts appear to be related to larger speech units like change of topic, beginning or ending of longer utterances, and so forth. These units of speech in turn are related to the way the speaker sorts out his thoughts, organises them, and forms them into words. Thinking on one's feet while talking in conversational situations lays the groundwork for all sorts of "nonverbal behaviour." It is nonverbal in that it does not consist of words, but it is directly influenced by the very act of talking.

A different organisation related to speech concerns the mechanics of changing speaker turns from one person to another. A large number of behaviors is involved in this system, from the rhythmical packaging of the speech itself and the concomitant grammatical structure to changes in eye contact (or head orientation), to certain gesticulatory behaviours and a number of others.

In the descriptions of other languages, one of the easily recognisable features of words and signs was that they referred to concepts that members of the language community had agreed were to be used to represent their various thoughts, ideas, feelings, and impressions. In the case of body language, some of the acts and postures have similar referents, and it will be instructive to go over the list again to see what the nature of those referents may be. Again, research findings will be the basis for the interpretations.

Among the discrete, categorical behaviours, emblems clearly have the most specific referents. Some of them are truly arbitrary, just as words are, and their referents may vary from culture to culture. The airman's sign for "A-OK," for example, used by United States astronauts and seen worldwide on television, is interpreted in some quarters as an obscene gesture. There are probably not more than a dozen or two of these arbitrary emblems in common use in the United States today. Many more of obvious pantomimic origin, the hitchhiker's thumb, for example, or the index finger to the lips for "shhh!" have referents that are just as specific as the arbitrary emblems. The movements that Birdwhistell has termed "kinesic markers," should probably also be included among the emblems as having quite specific reference. Whether all of these should be considered parts of body language as that term is popularly intended is an open question.

The two main functions of nodding, the signal that the listener is keeping up and the specific "Yes" substitute, have already been mentioned. Frequent nodding, when this movement is thus made into a continuous variable, would seem to be a sign of friendliness, but it has not always turned out that simply in research studies: it seems also to be the *result* of a friendly atmosphere. Frequent smiling definitely indicates a wish to be friendly and to be accepted by the other person, a finding quite in line with anyone's expectations. Eye contacts are timed in conversation to help regulate whose turn it is to talk: a person who is about to begin talking will look away from his conversational partner, and he looks back toward the end of rhythmical units of speech as if to seek the feedback that an "m-hm" or a nod would provide. The total length of time that a person looks at another during a conversation is associated with several variables: women look more than men, people attracted to each other look longer, extraverts look more than introverts, and so on. Staring at another is an upsetting stimulus, possibly an aggressive one (it is definitely aggressive in other mammals), from which the recipient will usually wish to escape.

The two postures, arms akimbo and the open position of arms and legs, are used by people interacting with others of lower status. In addition, the akimbo position is more likely when one is with someone whom one dislikes. Forward lean, as might be expected, occurs more among people who like each other. A more complicated pattern has been found with both distance and body orientation in ordinary conversational situations: one feels more comfortable at a greater distance and greater angle of orientation when dealing with a disliked person; he can be closest and oriented at the most direct angle with a neutral person, and somewhere in between with someone he likes.

Discretely performed hand movements (the gesticulations accompanying speech) are organised according to their relationships to speech rhythms. They occur more frequently at times when the flow of speech is interrupted by hesitations, "ahs," retraces, and other fumblings. These nonfluencies are far more frequent than we realise, since the listener very kindly edits them out as he tries to follow what the speaker is saying. So nonfluent passages have more gesticulating associated with them than the fluent. When these movements are treated as continuous information by counting them over longer periods of time, they take on another, less specific meaning. A person who gesticulates a great deal may be seen as having Mediterranean background, where people are known to gesticulate a lot, for example, or if his family is obviously not from one of those countries, as being nervous and high strung.

Among the behaviours called possibly discrete, organisation does not play much of a role since the behaviours are not made up of constituent parts in the same way as arms akimbo. The meaning is fairly clear and similar for all of these behaviors: people who lean forward toward their conversational partners, who stand close (but not too close for comfort), and who face squarely (but not completely so) are seen as friendly and warm.

The truly continuous behaviours are even less specific as to meaning. One does not know for sure, for example, if a person engaged in adaptor movements, such as stroking one hand with the other, is upset right now in this immediate situation or if he is inclined to move this way all the time. The same applies to rhythmical movements like swinging the feet and drumming the fingers. They provide information that must be interpreted in some way, not information that carries its own interpretation as discrete categories of behaviors like words and signs do.

As a matter of fact, this differentiation of the sort of information given by continuous and discrete behaviours may be applied to the whole list of movements given in this exposition of body language. The discrete, categorical movements, those that were listed as the most likely candidates for elements in a body language system, were also the most specific as to "meaning," in that the members of the community agree on what they refer to. They are thus the items with the highest information density. As the list progressed toward continuous behaviours, or as discrete behaviours were treated as continua by counting their frequencies over longer periods of time, more broadly probabilistic statements had to be made and phrases like "is associated with" began to crop up. The information density of these types of movement is lower. And these behaviours turn out to constitute most of the movements we see in social situations such as conversations.

With a few exceptions, then, we cannot look at a person's movements and know definitely what they mean in body language, the way we can see a series of signs in ASL (American Sign Language) and know the concepts they refer to. We must rather make probabilistic statements about them. If there are enough movements to yield enough probabilistic statements, we can feel more satisfied with our accuracy. In short, we can observe movement cues and make inferences from them about what is going on in the person we are observing, about what he is feeling, what his intentions are, and so on. These inferences cannot be couched in very specific terms, the way one might paraphrase what someone has said-that is, the precision of the conclusions we can draw from our inferences is not very high-but they can still serve us quite well in dealing with others day by day.

The conclusion in the last paragraph implies that the probabilistic statements were made up from individual, isolated events, like unconnected lists of words rather than sentences. But the topic here is organisation in body language—is there no organisation into larger chunks of meaning here, comparable to the sentences of spoken language or ASL? From what is available in current thinking and research, the answer to that question would have to be "No." People "say" things about themselves in body language, but not in the form of statements that could be part of any discourse. What they say, or what is available to others to "read," has a certain unity to it, to be sure, in that it does not consist of isolated events, but the interrelationships come from the basic state a person finds himself in at any given time, from which all his behaviors derive, not from the connectedness of any syntax such as that which relates words together in sentences.

By stretching a point one could find a few systematic relationships: for example, eye contact and distance are inversely related, probably because of the implications both have for intimacy. A sort of balance is struck, apparently such that if two people are standing or sitting very close to each other, they look at each other less than they would from a greater distance. In the case of emblems, usually more than one is needed to get a point across: letting someone know of a mock astonishment at hearing a piece of gossip might entail producing the "surprise" facial expression followed by a wry smile. But longer discourse could take place only under the most artificial circumstances even with emblems and probably not at all with other sorts of movement. Finally, the relationships among all of the behaviours that are involved in changing speaker turns include messages in body language. These messages do not make up any discourse in and of themselves, but rather contribute to a larger system of social interaction.

Summary: Body language as a limited system of communication. Here we have examined body language from the standpoint of its membership in the family of coded communication systems, and found it to qualify in only a few of its features. Discrete behaviors, performed in much the same way each time they appear, like emblems and a few postures, have meanings that everyone in the language community can agree upon. Most movements are not of that type, however, and they take as their organizing principles either the rhythmical structure of the concurrent speech, or their association with the state of being of the person, either long-term or situationally influenced. We use these less specific behaviours as cues to make inferences about those states in the person, and the success of those inferences varies with a number of factors. Extended discourse in body language, parallel to that possible in spoken language or ASL, does not seem to occur.

How much do we use movements to "Read" People?

The conclusion that body language is only a limited method

of communicating may be a disappointment, but it should not come as news. It should also not be construed as a death-knell for body language, for we do take in movements as we interact with other people, and we do make inferences from them. The question of how much we use them cannot be answered fully at this stage in the development of the field of social interaction because virtually no research has been done on that aspect of the problem. Still, some quite well-informed speculations can be made even now, and as long as they are recognised for what they are, as speculations, they can serve very well until more facts come in—even guide research efforts to find those facts.

The speculations derive from another field of psychology, that of perception, and more specifically from the thinking and work of D. E. Broadbent. He found that what gets through our perceptual apparatus, or what we attend to, depends on a number of features of the stimuli before us, as these relate to a specific characteristic of the perceptual apparatus itself. This characteristic is its limited capacity to handle information. It can deal with so much and no more. When we say that we cannot attend to two things at once, that is only partly true: what we cannot do is exceed the capacity of the system. Given two stimuli, the apparatus gives preference to: (i) the one whose information density is the higher, and (ii) the one with the greater intensity.

The application to conversations is clear: the speech

we hear, being of high information density, plus any of the more highly coded body language events, are likely to get through at the expense of any other less completely coded activities that may be going on at the same time. The intensity feature becomesleavener that allows body language material to pass the perceptual apparatus. Non-coded body language events that are intense enough will override the attention demandingness of the coded. Or a long succession of them can add up suddenly and make an impression, when for some reason attention becomes available.

The reasons attention might become available are many. There are fairly frequent lulls in conversations during which we do not need to concentrate on decoding the speech of the other person or on encoding into speech what we are trying to say. In addition, the conversation is not always about something we are eager to hear about, so we find our minds wandering.

Likely, the wanderings take us to preoccupations from earlier times or to plans for what we are going to do next, but attention could turn at those times to the less densely packed information in body movements. And we need not simply become bored to have attention available for lower information messages: some topics of conversation are inherently more difficult to grasp, and demand a good deal of brain power of all sorts, while others are much simpler, and some parts of most people's talk about them are highly predictable. The amount of attention paid to body language, then, varies from moment to moment, and we get intermittent chances to glimpse at the lower information movements from which we might make inferences about the people with whom we are dealing.

These are fairly solid lines of speculation about how body language can serve as communication, even those aspects of it that have relatively low information density. Very little of it can be read as specifically as the words and signs of the more completely coded languages, but often we do not need that degree of specificity: if we keep observing, hard as that may be when we are trying to keep up with a conversation, we will find more such messages and be able to get more out of the total communication situation. We may even be able to train ourselves to be increasingly alert to body language, though there are no research results yet available that would tell us how successfully we could do so. Perhaps that should be the next step for researchers to take.

Different body parts and their role in communicating

The Eyes

Eye Level: In a group, the person whose eye level is highest is usually perceived as the leader. Standing while others are sitting puts you in a definite position of authority.

Eye Rubbing: When a person strokes the eye with a forefinger, it indicates deception. Since this person wants to cut off visual contact, it provides an excuse for looking away. This usually involuntary movement is a dead giveaway that the person is not telling the truth.

Averting the Eyes: This is usually a sure sign of deceit, guilt or lying.

Closed Eyes: When someone's eyes close for a moment longer than a conventional blink and the eyebrows are raised, the message is, "Stop what you are saying."

Eyes Rolling Upward: This is a sign of exasperation.

Sideways Glance: This gesture is a coy, flirtatious signal. The person stares boldly while lowering the head and tilting it away — a classic move. It indicates "bold shyness".

Prolonged Glance: This is an unmistakable sign of sexual attraction. A person who makes eye contact, looks away, and then catches your eye again is saying, "I want to get to know you better."

Hard Stare: This signals an invasive, aggressive and threatening mood.

Up-and-Down Gaze: When a man runs his eyes up and down a woman's body, he's letting her know he's interested in a physical way.

The Wink: A wink is a deliberate signal. It shows that a secret is being shared between the winker and the one being winked at.

Both Eyebrows Raised: From across a crowded room, the signal is perfectly clear, "I want to meet you."

One Eyebrow Raised: When one eyebrow is raised and the other lowered, this means "I don't quite believe you."

Eyebrows Knit: When both eyebrows are drawn together, causing a furrow in the middle, it indicates acute anxiety, pain, fear, anger or a combination of these emotions.

Covering the Face: When the hand goes over the face it means, "I am shocked." The gesture distances the person making the gesture from an offending situation.

The Nose

Nose Touch: When a person's hand makes contact with his or her nose during conversation, it usually indicates that the person is hiding something. The person performing the action is usually unaware of the gesture and to all outward appearances, he or she seems calm. But inside, the person is actually in turmoil. Psychologists believe that touching the nose is an involuntary move to cover the mouth — and to hide the lie. But the hand shifts to the nose instead to disguise the meaning.

Nose Flare: Anger, exasperation or outrage.

Nose in the Air: When the nose is raised by tilting the head back, the message is clear. This person is saying, "I'm superior. I'm better than you." Literally, "looking down one's nose" is the universal symbol of snobbery.

Holding the Nose: Something is rotten.

Nose Twist: A nose twisted to one side indicates disapproval or dislike.

Nose Wrinkle: When the muscles around the nose tighten, creating wrinkle lines between the eyes, it reveals disgust — from mild disapproval to complete revulsion.

The Hands

The Firm Handshake: A person who reaches out and then turns the hand so that his or her hand is on top — palm down — is trying to dominate. This handshake is often used in diplomatic or political situations.

The Bone-Shattering Handshake: Indicates mastery and enthusiasm. There's no mistake who's in charge here.

Limp-Wrist Shake: A person who extends only the fingers or whose hand feels like a wet fish when you grasp it is saying, "I don't want to touch you; I don't like intimacy." It's also a sign of submission and weakness. When a man uses this handshake in a business setting, he may be indicating that he intends to secretly manipulate the situation.

Double Handshake: When the left hand is used to cover he hand being shaken, it is called the "glove handshake".

It shows an ultra-friendliness and intimacy — almost like a miniature hug.

Finger Motion: Tapping, strumming or keeping a steady rhythm with your fingers indicates impatience or a lack of tolerance. It's a symbolic form of running away — the fingers do the walking even though the body stays put.

Hands Hidden from Sight: This is a sly and secretive gesture. The person is saying, "I don't want to communicate with you." This is especially true for hands that are thrust deep into pockets where there can be no touching, hand-holding or any kind of intimacy.

Hands on Lap: When palms are up, the person is open and receptive. When palms are down, there may be aggression or deceit involved.

Finger Steeple: When someone presses the fingers together and rests the chin and mouth on the fingertips, it indicates deep thought — as though the person is praying for an answer. It is also a barrier that protects the chest, lower face and mouth.

Fist Covered by Open Hand: A person in this position is furious but struggling to stay calm — literally trying to "get a grip". But beware of this person — it may take very little to cause a loss of control.

Hands Jabbing: A person who wants to impose his or her ideas in a forceful manner may jab a hand toward the listener. A less aggressive action is to use only the forefinger.

Hands Clasped behind the Head: This is an arrogant gesture, especially if the person is leaning back. It says, "I have so much power over you, I don't even have to defend myself."

Fiddling with a Wedding Ring: This nervous trait indicates that there is something wrong with the relationship — especially if the person is talking about his or her spouse at the same time.

Fidgeting with Hands: This is the body's attempt to escape. The adrenaline is rushing but the person doesn't know how to get away. Playing with shirt cuffs or jewelry on the wrists tells others you need attention. In a bar, this action is appropriate. But in a business meeting, it's a distraction.

Stroking a Tie: This is a man's way of saying, "I'd like to make a good impression." It's his way of letting you know he's trying hard to please.

Hand through Hair: When people don't know what to say, they often run their fingers through their hair. The observer who can read body language knows the person is unsure about what to do or say next.

The Arms

Flexing the Arm: This says, "I'm strong." Raising one's arms also is a way of attracting attention. Reaching out with both arms is a gesture of welcome.

Arms Behind: When the hands are clasped behind one's back , it means the person has the situation under control They're saying "I'm at ease." It's similar to the pose that soldiers adopt when they're not at attention.

Arms in Front: When we're anxious, we tend to keep our hands and arms in front of our bodies to create a protective barrier.

Arms Clasping: Unlike arm crossing, where arms are crisscrossed over the chest, this gesture is seen when people are in anxious situations. It actually looks a if they are hanging onto themselves for dear life.

Arms Folded: When the arms are crossed in front of the body, it usually indicates a defensive posture. The person is saying, "I don't want to listen to anything that conflicts with my opinion." Most people are unaware of the barrier this stance creates, but it does serve to block any intrusion, especially if tense lips and a frown accompany it.

Spreading Out: When a man sits and spreads out, he's saying, "I'm taking over here." But when a woman does it, men tend to think she is overstepping her bounds. However, is she only places one arm on a neighbouring chair, she says, "I want to be equal to you."

Hands on Hips, Arms Spread (Akimbo): When the hands are placed on the hips so the elbows jut away from the body, the person is saying, "Stay away from me." This is an unconscious action that we perform when we're feeling antisocial or we're in a crowd and don't want others coming too close.

Shoulder Shrug: The shoulders hunch and hands are turned palms out. The message is clear, "I don't know you" or "I can't help you." It indicates a feeling of helplessness on the part of the person making the gesture.

The Legs

Jiggling the Foot: When a person is seated with legs crossed and one foot bouncing in the air, the message is, "I'm bored." These movements indicate running away, even though the person's body remains stationary.

Legs Crossed at the Knee: This familiar posture — equally popular among men and women — means, "I am very relaxed."

An Ankle over the Knee: This is normally a "guy thing". It says, "I am assertive but relaxed." This pose was the original "cowboy's leg cross". If you do it in a Middle Eastern country, don't let the sole of your shoe show!

Legs Crossed at the Ankle: This pose, used more often by men than by women, says, "I am politely relaxed."

Leg Twine: This is a popular pose for females. A women

entwines her legs, often hooking one foot behind her other ankle. Men find this difficult if not impossible to do. The tightness of the position gives the impression of self-hugging and adds a sexual overtone.

Locking the Foot: This is another gesture that is typically female. She stands and locks one foot behind the other. It usually means that she is nervous or uncomfortable.

Posture

Sitting: Do you know any sprawlers? These space invaders open their legs and drape their arms on the backs of neighbouring seats. They're broadcasting to everyone that they're in the room, filing it up with their presence.

Legs Crossed over Thigh: This is a typically masculine position that is also used by women who are wearing pants. It's an attitude that conveys stubbornness and means, "I won't change my mind, so don't bother trying."

Leg Hugging: Women do this more than men. They often settle on a chair or couch and curl into a tight ball hugging their legs. Although this self-loving attitude makes it seem as though a women is pulling inward, she is actually reaching out for a romantic encounter.

On the Edge of the Chair: When a person perches on the edge of a chair, you can assume the person is alert, opinionated and eager to share ideas and feelings — although they may be quite different than yours.

Clasping the Knees: When someone leans forward and clasps

the knees, that's a signal for you to talk fast. The listener is about to spring out of his or her seat and leave.

Straight-Backed: Determined, rigid and persistent is the message of people who sit like this. Maintaining appearances is important to them and they're willing to sacrifice almost anything to achieve their goals.

Leaning Backward: Also known as "chair-tippers", these are people who are adventuresome and mischievous. They're willing to take risks — like tipping over backwards, which sometimes happens.

Leaning Forward: Sitting in this posture shows intense interest in the speaker. It says, "I'm paying attention" When this happens, the speaker is often leaning backward, which indicates that he or she is in control.

Slumping: While it may appear that a person slumping in a chair is uncomfortable, the opposite is true. This informal attitude shows self-confidence in any social setting.

Both Feet on the Ground: These down-to-earth sitters are independent, practical and organised. They want you to know they're in command of the situation. The message these people give off is, "Watch your step around me. I mean business."

Chair Straddling: Turning the chair around and sitting as though astride a horse is typically masculine. It reveals a forceful and domineering person When a woman assumes this posture, she is saying, "I want to be like a man."

The Body

Stand Tall: An erect posture says you are self-assured, honest and successful. Even if you're short, a confident pose will make you appear more imposing.

Big Steps vs. Little Steps: Using the entire leg to walk, taking long strides and holding the back straight and head up indicate an assured, forthright attitude. Conversely, taking mincing steps with shoulders hunched makes a person appear timid and vulnerable.

Friendly Greeting: Briefly lifting an eyebrow when you first meet someone makes you seem interested, lively and alert.

Close Encounters: Everyone is entitled to a certain amount of personal space around them. As a rule, that personal space extends from three to six feet around you. The intimate zone extends a mere 20 inches. When a person moves in too close, it can cause discomfort. It is an aggressive move that shows little respect for the boundaries of others. This behavior can make a passive person feel vulnerable and defensive. Stay back — unless you are invited in.

Not Interested: If you want to seem above it all, lean back against a wall with your arms crossed over your body. The message is very clear — "Don't bother me."

Clamping the Neck: When the hand swings up and clamps itself to the back of the neck, it indicates anger. In primitive times, that gesture would have ended up as a swat or a bang on the other person's head. But in polite society, the action is checked. Those who know body language understand the power of this action.

Fidgeting: In a social situation, if you jingle the change in your pocket, play with your hair or fiddle with your clothing, it's a clear sign that you are nervous and tense. To make a good impression on others, try to calm these agitated motions.

Pulling the Pants: This is done more by men than by women, simply because men almost always wear trousers. The cloth of one leg is lifted to indicate disbelief, as though the person has just stepped in something distasteful and is trying to shake it off.

Leaning against the Wall: When you rest yourself against a wall or doorway in a relaxed and open way, you're saying, "Don't leave." It's a way of prolonging a conversation — especially if you're in a social setting.

Mirroring: When two people are talking and find themselves in the same position, it reveals a mutual fondness. People who have been together a long time often mirror each other's gestures and even say the same words at the same time.

Face Off: Unlike mirroring, which also occurs with two people face-to-face and body-to-body, it indicates extreme aggression. Under normal circumstances, people turn slightly away from one another when they're talking. If they want a showdown, however, they position themselves nose-to-nose in this very confrontational stance.

Bowing: This old-world gesture of respect is no longer typical in this country except in diplomatic circles and formal circumstances. In earlier times, however, it was used as a common greeting. Now it is most often used when actors or performers take a stage bow.

Various Gestures and Postures of Body Language

Human expression, sometimes mysterious and complex, sometimes simple and basic, is always a perfect unity. Some of us express ourselves in a pragmatic way, others creatively. Some reactions may be spontaneous, others elaborately planned. Yet, every reaction is an automatic combination of mind and body linked in a perfect partnership.

We humans may look very much alike to a citizen from another planet but in our own eyes, we are unique. When we study body, mind and movement, we are defining our unique differences of expression.

We think of the mind as an independent source of thought and inspiration. The physical participation of our body in our mental processes is less obvious to us.

Try this: close your eyes. Concentrate on feeling the

movement of your body as you breathe. You may become sensitive to the sounds outside, the temperature of the room, the position of your arms and legs, which you may not have noticed before.

Through our bodies we perceive our environment and instantly interpret it. For example, a hungry body keeps the mind focused on food; the sound of an animal moving in the bushes rivets your attention; you catch a falling crystal vase and save it from smashing.

Often when we close our eyes and relax, our minds wander to chores, memories or imagined dialogues. We are all familiar with this process. We know that the mind is free to roam unfettered by practical needs; I can travel to China in my thoughts and not need any transportation, visa, money or luggage. I am free to imagine anything I want, without limit. The body, while not as fanciful a traveler, is a reliable indicator of the workings of the mind.

Thus, by observing the body we can gain access to hidden thoughts and beliefs, even to patterns of behaviour in which we function but which are locked away in storage, operative, but out of awareness.

The body expresses feelings in different ways: a flick of an eyebrow; a jump for joy; a clenched fist. It takes complex coordination of body and mind, postures and gestures, to permit us to look meek and fearful; to look bold and tough. The body/mind process works together conscientiously. The partnership is so perfect it allows us to know what we want and organize to act in appropriate ways.

From the first awareness of a desire or need we organise our resources, our talents, our training towards satisfying that need. We get help from friends or professionals, so that we can take each step, grow, and fulfill the blueprint of our lives. If we have difficulty applying our energy toward accomplishing our goals, we can look for clues by examining movement. Old patterns may be continually repeating. The pattern could become a static physical posture, bringing rigidity into the process; into a relationship, into work habits and self-images.

When this happens, verbal information is inadequate. It continually describes the existing condition without progressing. Analysing a situation using words alone loses much of the variation of feeling and subtlety of the situation. It is like trying to tell the color of a flower from the seed. Movement will have the richness of color, texture and shape to provide the additional information we need.

The word 'mind' can have a global meaning: the consciousness of human-kind, the collective unconscious, the Mind of the Universe. In our usage here, the word "mind" encompasses the body. The body becomes a way of entering into various states of mind. We can change our "mind" through attention to the body.

The body and mind are always in total, instantaneous touch with each other. The body represents us in our journey through time and space. With body and mind working together as partners we are free to explore our life circumstances, who we are, what opportunities we have, what we can create, what we can discard. We are free to experience ourselves and others. We are beginning a journey of understanding and change.

Gestures and postures go hand in hand

Gestures and Postures are the frequent, continuous movement changes that happen in the body while speaking, walking, even sleeping. It is critical to understand the differences between postures and gestures in our study of movement. Postures are the activity of the whole body at once.

Postures are the more static and unchanging aspects of movement; they provide us with stability and consistency. They reinforce our behaviors such as: *"I am friendly, thoughtful, lively, cautious." "I am a good mother, friend, lover." "I am successful, wealthy, unhappy, dejected."* We have taught ourselves to project certain attitudes and we recognise ourselves in these postures. Postures develop from parental attitudes in upbringing, from role-models and from reactions to life events. We copy and learn postures. We store these in our bodies and use them to convey our desires and intentions. Postures are reactions to beliefs and statements of others as well as projections of our own beliefs.

Gestures are different. They are the expression of

adaptations of *parts* of the body, not the whole body. Gestures are vital to us for ordinary activities like making our morning coffee, waving 'hello,' dismissing things with a shrug, and generally getting along.

Some gestures are like signatures, they are so completely, individually ours. They may look decorative, extraneous or merely silly, but invariably they are significant. They help us sequence our verbal communication and layer it with messages. We record this information at a glance and automatically adjust to it.

Whereas gestures establish and keep the beat between people, giving a coherent rhythm to communication, postures support communication and establish a common platform of meaning. Without this underlying coordination of movements, we would have a hard time communicating.

We do not consciously keep track of these rhythms or shapes because we do not need to, but we should recognise them and understand what they represent. In these patterns we see compatibility, affiliations, group cohesion. There is as much under the surface of communication as there is above!

Since communication is what this book is about, take a moment now to do these easy exercises with a friend. You'll see, perhaps to your surprise, how often you use postures and gestures and how revealing they can be.

Discovering your personal postures and gestures

Gestures

Try mimicking a friend's gestures while maintaining a conversation. Become familiar with your friend's gestures.

Note how they enchance your understanding of the communication. Discuss them with your your friend and agree on their meaning.

Let your friend mimic your gestures. You are now creating a personal dictionary of gestures and their meaning.

Postures

Practice playing a role just for fun. Take on the arguments of your adversary. Feel your state of mind chan ge and be aware of how your posture changes

All about gestures

Each body part has its own way of moving. Each part transmits a signal, communicates, generates activity. Each part of the body can make learned, symbolic and expressive statements.

Close your eyes and picture a part of your body; for instance, your right hand. Move it around. See how it feels. As you move this part of your body, what might you be thinking, saying or doing?

Symbolic gestures

Most parts of our body are loaded with associations and meanings, sexual connotations, secret signs and standard messages. It is traditional to wave with a hand gesture; rub the stomach to say 'I'm full'; or spread the arms to welcome someone. Many gestures are cues between people to begin or end conversations.

Some gestures are signals. My father shakes his teacup to say, *"Fill it up, please"*; two therapists always light their pipes synchronously (unconsciously) before an important intervention. Families and groups establish rules which are enacted in gestures.

People attach personal meaning to their own gestures and learn to understand each other's. Thus, gestures both participate in the structure of communication and have personal meanings.

Functional gestures

We also use gestures to perform habitual tasks and chores which do not need our total physical or emotional commitment. With gestures we change the TV channel and water the plants. Any activity where we divide our attention and do more than one thing at a time, is done with gestures.

When we are unsure of ourselves we test the situation by using gestures. *"Do you mind if I sit here?,"* we say with a point of the head, when we need to share a table at a cafeteria. *"Let me try that,"* we say as we take over putting carrots into a new food processor. Movement, when it is being learned, is a series of gestures. Grace and ease come later, with the confidence that a movement can be performed safely and freely.

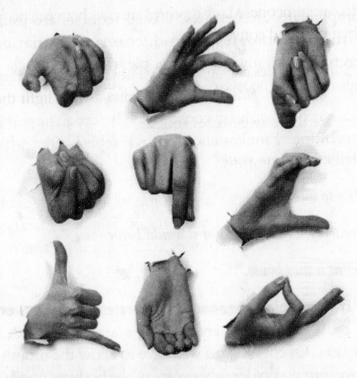

Some skills only demand gestures. For instance, an experienced knitter can easily knit and watch television at the same time. An adult doing a puzzle needs only a small gesture to insert a piece, while the child, less practiced, uses her whole body, showing a greater degree of involvement.

Gestures are the main units of communication. There

are more gestures in everyone's repertoire than any other kinds of movement. And the number and variety of gestures differs greatly.

Social use of gestures

Compliments are gestures. Casual requests are usually gestures. Apologies, introductions, explanations, directions, narratives about people, places or things are important and necessary gestures.

Here are the way gestures sound:

"Hello. How are you?"

"Nice to meet you."

"I'm sorry, I never thought it would bother you."

"What a nice house."

If you think the message of the statements is conveyed by the words alone, try making a statement with no gestures. Of course, you will have to allow the mouth to move, but do not let other parts of the body respond: no smile, no change in your eyes, no little bow of the head. You will find there is no way to totally neutralise the body except when the exchange is very mechanical, like requesting a train ticket or saying *"pass the salt."* Gestures accompanying verbal statements invariably offer additional information. *"Excuse me, do you have change for a dollar?,"* we ask as we offer the bill with a small movement of the hand and a bow of the head, apologetically. The gesture buffers the request and the stranger feels less threatened.

Sometimes when we are in a tense or uncomfortable position, an appropriate gesture has a positive effect. Saying *"I really have to go,"* with a glance at your watch helps break an overly long conversation. *"Hi, I can't talk now, I'm late for class,"* with a little skip away, helps us exit without feeling we have been abrupt.

Similarly, if you greet someone in a formal, Western cultural setting with no handshake, they will get the message that you wish to remain distant. It is a way of being cool without having to be impolite. Often we notice a gesture in the voice alone. The words: *"I'm fine"* can be said in a tone of voice dismissing any further discussion, implying *"Don't ask further."* *"I'm not fine but I don't want to discuss it right now."* Thus, gestures can directly contradict words. *"I love the gift,"* you say, without enthusiasm, or you raise an eyebrow to indicate that the words are not the whole story. You have leaked your true feelings. It might be preferable to say, *"I thank you for the gift. It was very thoughtful of you."* Your gesture is straightforward and you can mean what you say.

You can be sure the body will say what you feel, whether you want it to or not. Everyone feels more comfortable if what is said verbally equals what is said nonverbally. Choosing gestures carefully, you can be honest and polite.

Gestures in speeches and presentations

When delivering a speech, words alone do not convey the message. There must be a careful blend of appropriate expressive gestures to accompany the words. When gestures are too numerous, they can be confusing and distracting. The listener tends to pay more attention to the speaker's movement than to what is being said. For example, if the speaker fidgets and squirms while talking, he is engaged in a secondary communication with himself that has little to do with the text.

One can easily distinguish gestures that are referring to the self versus gestures which are going out to the audience, exposing the speaker's feelings and inviting communication. These are essential for a successful delivery. Even a brilliant text, if it is delivered with no audience contact, will most probably flop. Personal, communicative gestures are vital. Learned, rehearsed gestures are a disaster. Artificial gestures, which are not natural to the speaker, create a wall which keeps the audience from being able to empathise or even relate to the speaker.

Gestures can not only confuse an audience, they can confuse the speaker as well. A simple statement can become so embellished that it becomes unintelligible. When this happens, thoughts interrupt each other, comments are added to comments and the speaker loses track of content.

The quality of the gesture can give us valuable information about the personal style of the speaker, his feelings about the topic, or his feelings about the listener. Is the statement made with a sweep of the hand, as if the thought is being swept away, dismissed? Does it come with a jab, saying, *"Listen to this, it's important"* or *"I'm jabbing you, wake up!"* All this information is conveyed in gestures that accompany words.

The trouble with gestures

Gestures can interrupt our thought process. Your book falls to the floor. By the time you have picked it up, you've lost your idea. The idea has gotten shuffled up in the process of moving about. Take a deep breath, pause, and focus on one idea. Express it simply and clearly, vocally and in your body movement. Your voice will automatically sound like it is coming from your whole self. Stop. Say no more, You have now presented one thought with only the relevant gestures. Do not be tempted to say more. Pause. Wait, If necessary, present the next thought the same way.

Some gestures are associated with tension. These include scratching the head to enhance thinking or other semiconscious, repetitive gestures people use when they are *"lost in thought."* Tongue-chewing, nail-biting kinds of gestures all express tension in one part of the body. They can help us remain engaged in the task despite other concerns. Nervousness and discomfort can be personal habits or temporary reactions. On the positive side, this tension can protect us from a threat of, or real danger. If a gesture is simply a habit, we can attempt to eliminate it.

In a one-to-one situation, the use of numerous gestures (the result of complex feelings) can interfere with direct communication. Giving instructions to a new employee, you might find numerous gestures blocking good communication. Realising that every new employee needs simple guidelines in order to perform the job properly, you will need to clarify your expression.

Gestures alone are not powerful enough to change more complex emotional issues. Underlying attitudes have to be changed, needing a deeper commitment. Skilfully chosen gestures could start a process of change, but then the rest of the body must get involved if the change is going to be realised. Gestures can only describe the problem. But don't be discouraged, a gesture can lead you into a full commitment.

Postures: The Super-statement

You always have a posture of some kind, be it casual, accepting, or even neutral. It is a platform from which you can gesture. Your posture can change, all at once or bit by bit. You can stretch into a new posture as you relax from a cramped position or you can move limb by limb until a new arrangement is complete.

To see postures, picture the body as a shape emerging from its surroundings, its form making a continuous contour framed by, say, a chair, the wall or a window. Do not let your eye settle on individual parts but concentrate on the body as a sculpture outlined in space.

Postures set the mood

The whole body, arms, legs, hands, back and feet are arranged in a configuration which projects a mood or feeling: *"I am tired,"* can be seen in a drooping body, or, *"I am listening attentively,"* seen as a focused, alert body. The posture sets the mood. It remains the same even if there are gestures accompanying it, like doodling with a pencil, taking notes as I listen, turning my head to answer your question.

The mood you find yourself in is a result of the mental image you have. Your mood will vary and so will your posture depending on whether you are telling yourself that things are *"great!"* or *"terrible."* The mental image you have creates the state of mind from which you act.

Here's an exercise that will illustrate how posture creates a mood:

Picture yourself in a lovely setting; How does your body feel to you? Relaxed and at ease or tense and alert? How would it look to someone else? Does this mood make you more or less accessible to others?

To gain an awareness of your own postures, you need to be able to listen' to your thoughts, recognise the statement your thoughts would make and accept that your posture is participating in that statement. For example, if you are saying to yourself: *"That won't work, it's no good.,"* these critical thoughts will project in your posture. If you recognise this critical reaction and it is not what you want to project, you can choose to replace the critical thought with a non-critical one. Instead of *"That won't work,"* think *"What will work?"* Then you are in a helpful posture, looking for solutions. Communication is a two-way street. If it is not working, check out your postures and clear away the obstructions.

A second way to understand your posture is to actually feel it in your body and see it in your mind's eye. If you sense you are stiff, tense, holding back, see if there is something that you have not acknowledged that is causing this posture. Address the situation in a new way, rather than staying in a reactive posture. A new posture will form.

Suppose you have to attend the wedding of a distant relative on the very weekend you were planning to go to the beach. Your posture indicates annoyance and anger at your predicament. You create a fight with the nearest available person, just to give vent to those feelings. The fight leaves you feeling terrible and justifies your original frustration. So what do you do? Start by acknowledging the posture.

If, in fact, you must attend the wedding, set about replacing the attitude of frustration with a receptive one. Consider something positive you might gain from attending the event and allow yourself an appropriate posture. You are not fooling yourself, you are keeping an open mind. Choosing to change your body posture allows a larger perspective and more options. As a result, the situation will seem to adjust to you.

Below are five steps for mastering your own personal super-statements:

1. Become aware of your posture by listening to your thoughts.

2. Evaluate these thoughts for usefulness and effectiveness.

3. If necessary, construct a new attitude.

4. Feel the change in your body.

5. Use your body posture to help generate the positive feeling.

The best use of postures

As people begin to build rapport, they tend to adopt each other's postures. Even when this is momentary, it creates a matching of attitude which promotes ease in communication. As the relationship develops further, complementary postures continue to evolve.

It might look like this: while leaning down on the arm of a chair, one person might consider an issue, while the other person expands into the space brimming full of ideas. A poised, attentive posture helps some students learn, while a relaxed, casual posture helps others.

Salesmen know what reactions they are getting by being alert to the posture of the buyer. You can easily see which people in a group will be ready to participate by the availability seen in their posture.

You really need a posture when you have to object to something or defend someone. You may need to take a strong stand and you can only do it with a posture. A statement like *"Stop. That's wrong!,"* has to have a posture to match it or it is a helpless farce.

Postures are useful when practicing assertiveness or testing your position of power. Postures help charismatic leaders and spokespeople gain public support. Susan B. Anthony travelled and lectured throughout the United States and Europe in the mid 1800's insisting that women have the right to vote. Anwar Sadat risked his life promoting peace between Egypt and Israel. Martin Luther King, Jr. mobilised America against the injustices of segregation.

Preparing for conflict

Every relationship in work and family has its inherent status differences, personal and cultural. Some differences are fixed and some change. As the relationship changes, so do the postures. Postures naturally tend to match each other in a relationship of equals. In an argument, when postures match, they escalate the argument and make it hard to resolve. Hostility generates hostility; anger generates anger; rebellion promotes rebellion. Occasionally, in a relationship of equals, an apology for a mistake can take the wind out of the angry person's sails. Or, a bully may be shocked out of his or her bullying posture when he or she meets another bully. But when status conditions are not equal, postures generate their opposites. For example, rebellion in a teenager promotes a domineering posture in the parent; meekness promotes tyrannising; apologetic behaviour promotes accusative behaviour. In unequal status relationships like this, you must equal the posture of the accuser with your own, to show that you do not accept the blame or guilt.

The physical posture keeps the thought process held within its parameters. And so the posture reinforces the argument. The posture attempts to justify itself, not to change. Common complaints can become postures and generate defensive counter-postures rather than resolution. *"We don't spend enough time together." "You're always late." "You never do things right."* When you notice yourself thinking in these terms or you feel a fight brewing, think about your own posture and change it.

1. Physically put yourself in a new position. Move to a new chair. Stand. Sit. Relax your body. Change your arms and legs. Move.

2. Your mind is now ready to think along a different tack. Make your statement specific and talk about your own need or *fear.* *"This must be done right, and there are still errors. What are you going to do?" "If we don't make time for each other we will find ourselves out of touch."*

3. Do not expect an instant response. It may take time

for the other posture to dissolve. Let your statement rest and move on to other topics. The change has occurred. The results may come in later.

Your need alone may be compelling enough to generate understanding. You can stop here, or:

4.   Go on to spell out a solution which would suit you.

"I'd like to spend more time together. Let's go to the movies (a museum, a ball game, theater, etc.)"

In our relationships, we tend to focus on the other person's posture, but not on our own. We feel the other person has to change. Don't let a posture ruin your day. If it looks like it's a menace, get rid of it, any way you can. Laugh at it. Exaggerate it. Make it look ridiculous. The posture is potentially part of a chain reaction which elicits another posture. Before you know it, you are repeating the same old arguments. Instead, dissolve your posture and create a real solution.

Resolving Conflict

When a conflict sounds like this, postures are rushing out, tripping over themselves:

"You always undermine me when we are with other people" says Jane. (posture)

"No, I don't," responds Tom. (posture)

"You embarrassed me last night with Karen and Fred." (Jane intensifies her posture)

"You always criticize me." (Tom adopts a counter-posture)

We all know where this leads. Jane is taking a stand, exaggerating, generalising and hiding what is really bothering her behind a posture. Should Tom pursue proving her wrong? Definitely not! That would only serve to escalate the situation and make Jane even more determined to prove herself right. Instead, Tom might say:

"Do you really think I always undermine you? That's not my intention. Point it out to me next time so I can see what you mean."

Assuming the good will of both parties, Tom's understanding and restraint may help clarify the real issues here. Tom could match Jane's posture, the tone, quality, size and shape of it. But he need not defend himself verbally. If his posture matches her's, non-verbally he is saying: *"You cannot intimidate me with your loud voice and angry stance, but I will deal with what's bothering you."*

To understand your participation in a conflict or disagreement you may want to replay the exchange in your mind and think about the postures and gestures that took place. Were there antagonistic postures or threatening gestures? If you were attacked, did you assume a position of defence? Did your defensive posture keep you from expressing your view of the situation?

When emotions are intense and the stakes are high, a pre-arranged set of rules may be useful. One couple I know invented this one: no one could walk out on the relationship without giving the other twenty-four hours notice. (This allowed time for reconsideration and negotiation.) Other rules, like "equal time" or "no interruptions," can give people the chance to calm down and listen to the other's point of view.

Examples of different body gestures

BODY LANGUAGE	INTERPRETATION
Brisk, erect walk	Confidence
Standing with hands on hips	Readiness, aggression
Sitting with legs crossed, foot kicking slightly	Boredom
Sitting, legs apart	Open, relaxed
Arms crossed on chest	Defensiveness
Walking with hands in pockets, shoulders hunched	Dejection
Hand to cheek	Evaluation, thinking
Touching, slightly rubbing nose	Rejection, doubt, lying
Rubbing the eye	Doubt, disbelief
Hands clasped behind back	Anger, frustration, apprehension
Locked ankles	Apprehension
Head resting in hand, eyes downcast	Boredom
Rubbing hands	Anticipation
Sitting with hands clasped behind head, legs crossed	Confidence, superiority

Open palm	Sincerity, openness, innocence
Pinching bridge of nose, eyes closed	Negative evaluation
Tapping or drumming fingers	Impatience
Steepling fingers	Authoritative
Patting/fondling hair	Lack of self-confidence; insecurity
Tilted head	Interest
Stroking chin	Trying to make a decision
Looking down, face turned away	Disbelief
Biting nails	Insecurity, nervousness
Pulling or tugging at ear	Indecision

Portraying of Hands: Important Tool in Body Language

A life without hands is unthinkable. From scratching an itchy nose to carving up a juicy slice of prime rib to patting a grieving friend on the shoulder or earning your living – what would we do without them?

Of course the most basic and essential uses of hands are obvious – we must feed ourselves, take care of personal hygiene, put on our clothing, drive ourselves where we want to go – or in some cases let our thumbs arrange transportation – we create beauty with paint and marble, metals and gems; we communicate through any number of electronic gadgets – busy little fingers punching in words and numbers, darting here and there doing this and that – constantly performing the services and tasks that make up our lives.

But there is another aspect to our hands that we over

look or perhaps aren't even aware of – and that's the silent communication of our hands in a hundred subtle ways.

We throw them up in supplication or self-defence; we extend them in peace or comfort or an 'open-handed' invitation; we hide them when we seek to hide our real thoughts or truth; we clench them in anger or fear and wring them in worry grief or greed. Some of us even nibble on the ends of them when we are deep in thought or agitated. We demonstrate our nervousness or guilt and usually we are not even aware of it.

Various hand gestures and their meaning

One hand gestures

Itching under the chin

In Italian culture this represents "I don't care, I can't be bothered". This is done by keeping one hand straight, placing it under the chin, and 'throwing out' that hand toward the person receiving the gesture. In Italian and American culture this represents "Screw You!"; U.S. Supreme Court justice Antonin Scalia received criticism for using this gesture towards a reporter.

Scratching or stroking the chin or beard (where possible) can be used to indicate that the gesticulater is thinking or puzzled. In the UK, an "itchy chin" can be used to indicate that the person receiving the gesture is lying or talking nonsense, bullshit, in other words. In the

UK scratching the chin as a way of implying that the speaker is talking nonsense is often accompanied with any or all of the phrases "reck-on", "chinnus magnus" and "jimmy hill" in no particular order.

Beckoning sign

Index finger sticking out of the clenched fist, palm facing the gesturer. The finger moves repeatedly towards the gesturer (in a hook) as to draw something nearer. It has the general meaning of "come here", although it is normally seen as condescending or anyway impolite. It is sometimes performed with the four fingers, with the entire hand, or even with the arm, depending on how far the recipient of the sign is.

When performed with the index finger, it may have a mild sexual connotation depending on the circumstance. In Africa, the Far East and many Spanish-speaking countries, this sign is given with all four fingers and with the palm down.

In Japan there is a similar gesture, but the four fingers are used, the palm faces the recipient and the hand is at head's height. This is the gesture featured in the maneki neko.

Benediction and blessing

The benediction gesture is a raised right hand with the ring and pinky fingers touching the palm, while the middle and index fingers remain raised. Taken from Ancient

Roman iconography for speaking (an example is the Augustus of Prima Porta where the emperor Augustus assumes the pose of an orator in addressing his troops), it is used as a simple charm or blessing amongst many modern Pagans, and has a vast array of uses. Perhaps the most common and/or noteworthy use of the gesture is while tracing an invisible "air pentagram" before someone during certain Wiccan rituals such as the Great Rite performed during Beltane and Drawing Down the Moon on the Esbats. One might also use the gesture to trace invisible pentagrams or other sigils over items to be blessed or empowered, such as holy water, ritual wine, ritual ale, or the Sacred Herb. The two extended fingers are used to point (except when an athame, wand, or sword is used).

A similar sign, called the *benediction* gesture, is used by the Christian clergy to perform blessings with the sign of the cross; however Christians keep the thumb raised - the three raised fingers (index, middle, and thumb) are frequently allegorically interpreted as representing the three Persons of the Holy Trinity. It was shown by representations of Jesus as Christ Pantocrator.

Check, please

This gesture, understood by waiters around the world to mean that a dinner patron wishes to pay the bill and depart, is executed by touching the index finger and thumb together and "writing" a wavy line in the air, as if to sign one's name. An alternate gesture with the same meaning is made by touching the index finger and thumb together and drawing a checkmark (?) in the air. In Egypt, the left hand is held palm-out and the right, palm-down, is tapped against the left wrist to request the check. In Thailand, one makes a circling gesture with the thumb and fingers pinched together- as if you are holding an imaginary pencil and making imaginary scribbles on a piece of paper. Sometimes the opposite palm is used as the 'paper'. In the Philippines, one outlines a rectangle in the air using the thumb and forefinger of both hands.

Crossed fingers

A gesture made by crossing the index and middle fingers such that the middle finger overlaps and intertwines the index finger, which can be used to signify one's hope that something should succeed (compare to the phrase "Keep your fingers crossed."). According to OldSuperstitions.com, this stems from the superstition that "Bad luck is trapped at the point where the two fingers meet so when we cross our fingers, we stop the bad luck from escaping and allow our wishes to come true.". However, if placed behind one's back, the gesture takes on an entirely different meaning: it is then normally used to indicate that the user secretly wishes for something *contrary* to what is being stated or going on, or that a lie is being told. This usage is often seen in dramatic contexts.

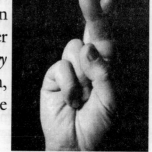

Cuckoo sign

A gesture made by closing ones fist, extending the index

finger, and circling it around ones ear for several seconds. This gesture is used to indicate that someone is speaking nonsense or is crazy (more colloquially, this is described as being cuckoo). The "cuckoo" sign is well-known in the United States.

Fig sign

The "fig sign" is a gesture made with the hand and fingers curled and the thumb thrust between the middle and index fingers, or, rarely, the middle and ring fingers, forming the fist so that the thumb partly pokes out.

In some areas of the world, the gesture is considered a good luck charm, in others it is considered an obscene gesture, and in still others it is used in the "I've got your nose!" child's game. This gesture is also the letter "T" in the American Sign Language alphabet.

In International Sign, which otherwise uses the same manual alphabet, "T" has been modified to avoid possible offense.

In ancient Rome, this gesture was called the *mano fico*, and was a fertility and good luck charm designed to ward off evil. Although this usage has survived in Brazil, where carved images of hands in this gesture are used in good luck talismans, in many other cultures, such as Greece, Indonesia, Turkey, Cyprus and Russia, the sign has come to have an insulting meaning n modern Russia this gesture is used mostly by kids with the meaning "screw you/no way". The same meaning is expressed by adults either with bent elbow (rude, very emphatic, non-classy), or with a "finger" (used mostly by city dwellers).

The "finger" made it to Russian gesture language from Western movies. In modern Italian, the gesture is called the *mano fica*, taken to mean "fig hand", as the Italian word for "fig" is *fico* (*ficus* in Latin). The obscene connotations of the gesture may partly originate from the fact that a similar Italian word, *fica*, is a slang term referring to the vulva. This sexual connotation may date back to ancient Roman times; some Roman amulets combine a *phallus* and a *mano fico* gesture. In Dante's *Inferno*, Vanni Fucci curses God with a "fig" gesture.

In some Balkan countries, particularly in the regions of Bosnia, Serbia, or Croatia, the "fig" sign is addressed as the "šipak", having the same connotation. In both contrast and comparison to the modern Russian "screw you/no way" meaning of the gesture, the sign is used, almost exclusively in situations aimed at being comical, to mean "nothing". For example, if one was to ask another person, usually a close affiliate, what they are to receive, either as a gift or something that the person expects the affiliate to give them, the affiliate would then form the šipak and present it in front of the other person (sometimes saying "šipak" as well).

While the modern Russian meaning is almost exclusively used among children, the gesture's meaning amongst the certain Balkan regions are used by, but not limited to, children, as adults have also been known to use the gesture either with another adult or with a child (usually their own) in a comical manner.

Also known as the Sicilian Fist in Sicily, worn as a good luck charm. Images of the "Sicilian Fist Charm" in Sicily. The gesture is also used in a trick played by adults and parents, with the intention of convincing their child that his or her nose has been taken away. Someone, usually an adult, grabs at the child's nose and forms the fig sign, exclaiming, "I've got your nose, I've got your nose!" The thumb is supposed to be the child's removed nose.

Many neopagans use this gesture as a symbol of the mother goddess to help adherents identify one another. In this context, it is referred to as the "Sign of the Goddess". Its counterpart is the *corna* sign.

In The Gnostic Mass of Aleister Crowley, this gesture is assumed by the priest throughout the Mass when his lance is not in his hand. It is a phallic device and symbolizes copulation, the fruit of which is a fig, traditionally appropriated to Jupiter the phallic sky god. The use of "the ficus" in the Gnostic Mass replaces the sign of benediction used in Christian ceremonies.

Finger snap

One of several gestures familiar to modern people primarily through old animated cartoons, this gesture generally expresses a confident "screw you!" in the face of an adversary. The gesturer holds one hand out, palm up, in the direction of his antagonist and snaps his thumb and middle finger, generally accompanied by a high-nosed, "snooty" facial expression and followed by crossing the arms.

In some countries, particularly Great Britain, snapping the fingers is used to signify remembering or failing to remember. Snapping the fingers repeatedly at a constant rate is commonly used to signify that the person has forgotten something and is trying to recall it. This is often done with the fingers snapped close to the temple, as though literally 'jogging the memory,' and is associated with the phrase 'it's on the tip of my tongue.'

A single snap, sometimes emphasized by an arced swing of the arm, is used when someone is reminded of something by another person, particularly if it is a job or a chore they have forgotten to do, or as a sign of disappointment or regret.

Some people also snap their fingers to catch the attention of others. This is informal – some people may find it rude or even threatening, as it is common for the gesturer to snap his fingers very close to the other's face. In some cases, this may be interpreted as a face-threatening act or a sign of contempt.

Finger snap

A single snap, sometimes emphasized by an arced swing of the arm, is used when someone is reminded of something by another person, particularly if it is a job or a chore they have forgotten to do.

Some people also snap their fingers to catch the attention of others. This is informal – some people may find it rude or even threatening, as it is common for the gesturer to snap his fingers very close to the other's face. In some cases, this may be interpreted as a face-threatening act or as a sign of contempt. In other cases, it may be a secret victory sign.

In a classroom, children may snap their fingers to indicate that they are eager to give the answer to a question.

It can also be used when telling a story, to get a surprise effect. In Latin America this gesture is used as a way to say "Hurry up." The Beats (Beatniks) used to snap repeatedly as more reserved "cooler" applause.

Fours snaps in the shape of the letter Z are used to convey superiority or disdain for all others. This is called a "Z snap".

How sad

This gesture (also called "Playing the World's Smallest Violin") is made by rubbing the thumb and index finger together. It is used to show lack of sympathy for someone telling a sad story.

I love you sign

Made using a combination of the letters 'I', 'L', and 'Y' from American Sign Language. It is made by extending the thumb, index finger, and little finger while the middle and ring finger touch the palm.

Index finger

Made with the palm forward and the index finger up, this is a warning sign ("watch out!") to a particular person (in western culture).

When made in a group of people, it is an indication that one wants to speak. Making a motion side to side with the index finger indicates the equivalent of "no, no".

Shaking the index finger toward the interlocutor and back several times, when used by adult toward the child, means "do not do this, I will punish you". This is known as "noo-noo-noo" gesture in Russia and in Israel.

Loser sign

This sign is made using the right hand by making a fist and an 'L' shape with the index finger and thumb. The back of the hand is then tapped against the forehead indicating that the recipient is a loser. This gesture is often followed with a double loser. The song All Star by Smash Mouth refers to this gesture: "She was looking kinda dumb with her finger and her thumb in the shape of an L on her forehead."

Middle finger

Former professional wrestler Stone Cold Steve Austin used the finger quite frequently in WWE shows. He raises both of the fingers to the crowd as a way of saluting to them.

Also, he gestures the finger at his opponent before kicking them in the stomach and performing the Stone Cold Stunner.

Comedian Dane Cook parodied the gesture with his "Super Finger" gesture, which consists of raising the middle finger, ring finger, and thumb on the same hand while lowering (or curling) the pointer and pinky finger. It is meant to be a more "powerful" version of "the finger".

The middle finger is also used to represent the number four when one counts in the binary system using one's fingers. When this gesture is made with the palm facing forward, it is known to Chaotes practicing Lovecraftian magick as the "Sign of Kish".

Another Lovecraftian sign is the "Sign of Koth", which consists of fully extending the index finger, middle finger, ring finger, and pinky, while the thumb is tucked against the flat of the hand.

Money sign

The thumb rubs repeatedly over the tip of the index finger and middle fingers. The ring finger and pinky touch the palm. This gesture is meant to resemble the act of rubbing two coins together (alternatively the act of counting paper bills) and has a general meaning of "money", or "expensive".

OK

This is the touching of the index and middle finger (or

just index finger) with the thumb (forming a rough circle) with the raising of the remaining fingers. In the United States and most of Europe, it means "OK" and is inoffensive. The OK sign is used extensively in scuba diving. It can also mean "0," or "money," in Japan. However, in Germany, it is often seen on the Autobahn, as a silent way of calling someone an "Asshole" (with the fingers extended horizontally).

Similar vulgar meanings are found in other countries, but usually you have to turn the 'Ring' upside down (supinated to show the ring in front) like this example from Brazil.

Palm of hand

In most places, a palm raised towards somebody means "stop". In Greece, the palm of the hand thrust towards somebody with the fingers splayed is an offensive gesture equivalent to giving the finger.

The gesture is known in Greek as "moutza". It originates from the Byzantine punishment of parading a chained criminal around town with his face smeared with cinder, or *moutzos* in Greek.

An even more offensive version is achieved by using both hands to double the gesture, and smacking the palm of one hand against the back of the other, in the direction of the intended recipient. Both the one-handed and the two-handed versions of this gesture can be (and often are) combined with the term "*na!*", meaning "here you go!" or "there!", or "*na, malaka*!", meaning "there, you wanker!" In Latin America, something similar is used. Except when the fingers touch the top of the palm as if one holds a baseball to throw a knuckball.

Patience

Palm up, index and middle fingers touching the thumb, remaining fingers folded against the palm, and wrist bending slightly, up and down about three times, so that the touching fingers move toward and away from the gesturer. This gesture is used as a reproachful and exasperated request for patience in response to a request to be served immediately out of turn or for something to happen faster than is possible.

Pointing

The typical pointing with the index finger is a gesture used in many cultures. Some cultures use the middle finger (certain regions of India) other cultures also point with the thumb, often when referring to something behind the speaker. There are many other ways to point, for example with the hand, a head nod or an eye gaze. In some Native American cultures, one actually points with the nose, avoiding the disrespect associated with pointing fingers. Some cultures use lip pointing, for instance the Misquite in Honduras and Nicaragua. In Western cultures pointing directly with the index finger at a person is considered rude. A more polite way of pointing to a person would be to direct the hand in their direction, as if holding a plate.

Raising a hand

Raising a hand is a gesture that conveys hello. This gesture is close to salute, and is also used in an audience when one wishes to speak or be recognised.

Salute

There are many forms of salute gestures, most of which are used to denote respect or obedience for an authority. A common military hand salute consists of raising the right hand, held flat, to the right eyebrow. Scouting organizations use related salutes. The armies of various countries adopt slightly different forms of salute: in the United States, the military salute places the hand directed outward over the eyebrow, like a visor; in the United Kingdom armed forces, the hand is brought to the forehead palm outward in military and air force contexts, whereas the naval salute is as in the US forces — the US forces derived their saluting habits from the Royal Navy.

One of the most infamous forms of salute is the "Hitler salute", which is performed by extending the whole right arm, palm outstretched and facing down, upwards into the air at approximately a 45 degree angle from the ground.

Sometimes, this is accompanied by holding the index

and middle fingers under the nose, representing Hitler's iconic moustache. This gesture is associated with Nazism and its leader, Adolf Hitler, as well as with Germany during World War II.

It is occasionally performed to mock someone or something for perceived authoritarianism or bigotry. This gesture was based on the Roman salute, and it was in that capacity that it was revived by French Revolutionaries and later by Benito Mussolini's Fascist party.

In some countries, mostly in Europe, it is forbidden by law to perform this gesture, although this does not deter Neo-Nazis and white supremacists from using the gesture in public rallies. Even in other countries, it is generally considered taboo to use the gesture, and this partly caused the United States to abandon the similar Bellamy salute used when reciting the Pledge of Allegiance, in favor of the current hand-on-heart gesture.

Shush

This gesture is used to demand or request silence from those to whom it is directed. The index finger of one hand is extended, with the remaining fingers curled toward the palm with the thumb forming a fist. The index finger is placed vertically in front of the lips.

Often, the lips will be formed as if to make a "shh" sound, whether or not a sound is made.

An alternate gesture with the same meaning involves the thumb and forefinger moving horizontally across the lips, as if one would be closing a zipper.

To further exaggerate on the action, some place their index finger and thumb together, curl the other fingers towards the palm and twist their hand in a fashion similar to locking a door. This is done after *zipping* the mouth and while their hand is still at the corner of their lips. Some may also imitate throwing the *key* away so as to show that the person should not open their mouths.

This action of *zipping* the mouth and throwing away the *key* to it may also take on the meaning of telling someone that you will keep your mouth shut about a secret.

Three middle fingers

Gestures consisting of fully extending the index, middle, and ring fingers with the thumb and pinky tucked together under the palm have had a variety of meanings over the years.

The gesture was also used by Bosnian Croats as a victory sign, representing the Christian Trinity, during the Bosnian War. To Chaotes practicing Lovecraftian magick, this gesture is known as the "Sign of the Elders." With the palm facing outwards, the fingers closed (without gaps), the right hand's fingertips to the same-side temple, it is used by the Boy scouts as their identifying salute.

In the United States, when the back of the hand faces outwards, this gesture is often used as a euphemism for "the finger." It is used especially when a jocular effect is desired. Originally, an accompanying verbal explanation was usual — "Read between the lines," referring to the common English expression denoting that one must read carefully to glean the subtle meaning in a passage — but this phrase is now commonly omitted.

Thumbs up, thumbs down

A closed fist held with the thumb extended upward or downward is a gesture of approval or disapproval respectively. These gestures have become metaphors in English: *"My boss gave my proposal the thumbs-up"* means that the boss approved the proposal, regardless of whether the gesture was made — indeed, the gesture itself is unlikely in a business setting.

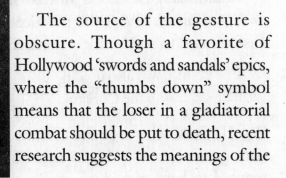

The source of the gesture is obscure. Though a favorite of Hollywood 'swords and sandals' epics, where the "thumbs down" symbol means that the loser in a gladiatorial combat should be put to death, recent research suggests the meanings of the symbols have changed over the years. In 1997, Professor Anthony Philip Corbeill of the University of Kansas concluded that the thumbs up actually meant "Kill him," basing his assertion on a study of hundreds of ancient artworks.

Thus, the "thumbs up" was an approval of the gladiator's request to kill his vanquished foe rather than a vote to allow the defeated to remain alive. Corbeill wrote that a closed fist with a wraparound thumb was the indication for a gladiator's life to be spared.

In Latin, the "thumbs up" gesture is called *pollice recto*, "thumbs down" is *pollice verso*. It is not certain that the contemporary gestures are identical to the gestures performed in ancient Rome. The current version was popularised by a widely reproduced academic painting by the 19th century artist Jean-Léon Gérôme, whose *Pollice Verso* depicts a triumphant gladiator standing over a fallen foe, looking up into the bleachers for the verdict of the crowd.

Additionally, Desmond Morris' *Gestures: Their Origins and Distribution* traces the practice back to a medieval custom used to seal business transactions. Over time, the mere sight of an upraised thumb came to symbolise harmony and kind feelings. The gesture's popularisation in America is generally attributed to the practices of World War II pilots, who used the thumbs up to communicate with ground crews prior to take-off. American GIs are reputed to have picked up on the thumb and spread it throughout Europe as they marched toward Berlin.

More recently, these gestures are associated with movie reviews, having been popularized by Gene Siskel and Roger Ebert in their televised reviews — the thumb up meaning a positive opinion of a film; the thumb down meaning a negative one. One or two thumbs up, often held over the head, may also be used by athletes in celebration of a victory.

'Thumbs up' traditionally translates as the foulest of Middle-Eastern gesticular insults — the most straight-forward interpretation is 'Up yours, pal!' The sign has a similarly pejorative meaning in parts of West Africa, South America, Russia, Iran, Greece, and Sardinia.

Hitchhikers traditionally use a thumbs up gesture to solicit rides from oncoming vehicles, although in this presentation the arm is generally outstretched with the palm and closed fingers facing the motorist. People who have the genetic ability to bend the tip of their thumb backwards are said to have "hitchhiker's thumb," which is a reference to the original gesture.

Talk to the hand

This gesture is used as a physical interjection to express indifference or contempt and interrupt what someone is saying. The arm is extended with the hand vertical and palm facing and centred around the face of the other individual.

V sign

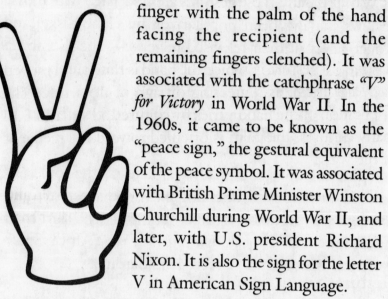

The "V sign" is made by lifting the middle and index finger with the palm of the hand facing the recipient (and the remaining fingers clenched). It was associated with the catchphrase *"V" for Victory* in World War II. In the 1960s, it came to be known as the "peace sign," the gestural equivalent of the peace symbol. It was associated with British Prime Minister Winston Churchill during World War II, and later, with U.S. president Richard Nixon. It is also the sign for the letter V in American Sign Language.

This sign is frequently used by the Japanese, most times holding up 2 "V" signs very close to either side of their face with a big grin during pictures.

In the UK, Australia, and some other countries, reversing the V sign so that the back of the hand faces the recipient is seen as the equivalent of giving the finger. Popular, but discredited, myth supposes it was originally a taunt by English longbow archers towards the French who were known to cut off an English archer's first and middle fingers if captured.

Additionally, due to its use in an advertisement for the Australian made Valiant Charger (which ceased production around 1980) many people still display the V sign, in homage to the ad and the car, if that vehicle happens to be driven past.

Wave

A wave is a gesture in which the hand is raised and moved back and forth, as a greeting or sign of departure. The orientation of the hand varies by culture and situation. In many cultures, the palm is oriented toward the recipient of the wave.

In Chinese culture, orienting the hand palm-down and waving it up and down signifies "come here", rather than a greeting.

Gestures using two hands

Asking for the time

Common in the United States, a silent way of asking someone else what time it is. One hand is usually clenched into a downturned loose fist, bent at the wrist, while the index finger on the other hand is used to tap the bent wrist as if pointing to a wristwatch.

Awkward turtle

The Awkward Turtle is a gesture made after something awkward just happened, or when there is an awkward silence. To perform an awkward turtle there are three steps to take. First, place hands on top of each other. Next, move thumbs out and away from the hands. Finally, rotate the thumbs. Nowadays the gesture is used in the United States to hush children, or to calm participants in a heated argument. In Japan, the same gesture may be used to request the check when dining at a restaurant.

"Gills"

This gesture involves holding the backs of the wrists against the jawline (with elbows outstretched) and then waggling one's fingers. The gesture is often accompanied by a feminine-voiced "Ooooo!" which rises and falls in intonation. It is used when one would normally say (sarcastically) "well aren't you clever?", or to imply that someone is acting too posh for their station. It is peculiar to Scotland owing to its use in Scottish TV sketch show Chewin the Fat.

"Shame on you"

This gesture involves pointing at a person with the index finger of one hand while rubbing the pointed finger with the index finger of the opposite hand. The rubbing motion is directed toward the intended recipient and is repeated at least twice. It is used to imply that the targeted person should feel shame.

In Flanders and also in the German-speaking countries, this gesture is used in children games to indicate "we got you/we're smarter than you/we laugh at you", often accompanied by the mocking sing-song "AhahahaHAha!" shouted out loudly.

Scream

The palms are against the sides of the face, eyes wide and

mouth open round. This gesture is depicted in Edvard Munch's The Scream. To imitate the painting, there may be a small space between the palms and the face. It is used to express great horror. With the mouth closed, it is used to express dismay. A similar gesture, placing the hands against the front of the face, little fingers parallel and touching, can express sadness, remorse, or speechlessness over any bad event.

Time-out

The "time-out" gesture — a "T" formed with the hands,  with one hand with flat palm placed perpendicular to the other hand with flat palm, roughly in the centre — originates in American sports. It is used by players to signal for a time out, or brief pause in play. In basketball, the gesture is additionally used by referees to indicate that a player or coach is guilty of a technical foul. In the Northern California Hyphy movement the gesture is known as "puttin' your T's up" and indicates a preference for MDMA, colloquially known as "thizz." The gesture was popularized by Hyphy icon Mac Dre, who was notorious for his use of MDMA.

In Portugal this gesture is used to say "Please give me some time" (or some more time).

(6)

Facial Expressions of Emotions

In just a moment or two, expression flashes on and off the face. Wrinkles appear where the skin was smooth, or permanent wrinkles momentarily deepen. The eyebrows, eyelids, and mouth temporarily change their shape.

Are these quick changes in the face expressions of emotion? How many emotions are shown on the face?

Are these expressions true indications of how a person feels, or can they be falsified? Are most people able to read accurately facial expressions?

What are the clues to emotion in the face; how is each feeling registered in the wrinkles and features of the face? Are the facial expressions of emotion the same for all people, or do they vary with culture, language, age, sex, and personality?

Which emotions does the face show?

Does the face tell us only whether someone feels pleasant or unpleasant, or does it provide more precise information, conveying which unpleasant emotion is experienced? If the latter, how many of these specific emotions does the face show—6, 8, 12, or what number? The typical method used to determine just which emotions can be read from the face has been to show photographs of facial expressions to observers, who are asked to say what emotion they see in each face. The observers may be given a predetermined list of emotion words to choose from, or left to their own resources to reply with whatever emotion word comes to mind. The investigator analyzes the answers of the different observers to determine what emotions they agree about in describing particular faces.

He might find, for example, that 80% of the observers agree in describing a particular face with the word "afraid." They might not agree about a word to describe some other face; for example, a face called "disinterest" by some observers might be called other emotions by other observers. On the basis of such results, the investigator reaches a conclusion about which emotions the face can convey.

The six emotions—happiness, sadness, surprise, fear, anger, and disgust-were found by every investigator in the last 30 years who sought to determine what emotions can be shown by facial expressions. There are probably other emotions conveyed by the face-shame, interest, and excitement, for example, but these have not yet been as firmly established.

Are judgements of emotion accurate?

It is not enough to determine what emotions are read from facial expressions. It is also crucial to discover whether the interpretations of the observers are correct or not.

When people look at someone's face and think that person is afraid, are they right or wrong? Are facial expressions an accurate reflection of emotional experience?

Or, are the impressions gained from facial expression merely stereotypes-all agree about it, but they are wrong? To study this question the investigator must find some people whom he knows to be having a particular emotional experience. He must take some photographs, films or videotapes of these people, and then show them to observers. If the observers' judgments of the facial expression fit with the investigator's knowledge of the emotional experience of the persons being judged, then accuracy is established.

In our analysis of all the experiments conducted over the last 50 years, we found consistent and conclusive evidence that accurate judgments of facial expression can be made.

Some of these studies were conducted in our own laboratory. In one experiment photographs were taken of psychiatric patients when they were admitted to a mental hospital and again when they were less upset and ready for discharge. Untrained observers were shown these photographs and asked whether each facial expression was shown at time of admission or at time of discharge. The judgments were accurate. These same photographs were shown to another group of observers who were not told they were seeing photographs of psychiatric patients but instead were asked to judge whether the emotion shown was pleasant or unpleasant.

Again accuracy was proven since the facial expressions shown at admission were judged as more unpleasant than those shown at discharge from the hospital. In another study other observers were asked to judge how pleasant or unpleasant the facial expressions were, but the faces shown to them were of psychiatric trainees undergoing a stress interview.

Without knowing which was which, the observers judged the facial expressions during stress as more unpleasant than the facial expressions drawn from a non-stressful part of the interview. In still another experiment observers were shown films of college students, taken when they had been watching a very unpleasant film of surgery and when they had been watching a pleasant travelogue film. The observers accurately judged which film the college students were watching from their facial expressions.

All of these studies were concerned with spontaneous facial expressions that naturally occur when a person does not deliberately try to show an emotion in his face. But what of those situations in which a person deliberately tries to show an emotion, to look happy or angry, and so forth? Many studies have found that observers can accurately judge which emotion is intended when a person deliberately tries to convey an emotion through facial expression.

How does each emotion appear on the face?

As we began to find evidence that there are some facial expressions of emotion that are universal, and before all of the studies were completed, we began to investigate just what these universal facial expressions of emotion look like. We sought to construct a tool for measuring the face, which would depict photographically each of the universal facial expressions of emotion. Our first step was to study what others had said about the appearance of the face for each of the primary emotions. Some writers had described which muscles were contracted in particular emotions, while others concerned themselves only with the appearance of the surface of the face. None had systematically considered all of the muscles nor all of the consequent changes in the surface appearance of the face for the six primary emotions.

Putting together what was written by Darwin, Duchenne, a French anatomist whom Darwin had quoted extensively, Huber, an American anatomist writing over 40 years ago, and Plutchik, an American psychologist concerned with emotion, we saw part of the picture emerge. We constructed a table that listed all of the facial muscles and the six emotions, entering into the table what these men had written about which muscles were involved in what way for each emotion. There were, however, many gaps, where no one had said anything about the involvement of a particular muscle in a particular emotion. Working with Silvan Tomkins, we filled in those gaps with information from our cross-cultural studies, and our shared impressions.

The next step was to photograph models who were

instructed to move particular facial muscles. We separately photographed the three areas of the face that are capable of independent movement: the brow/ forehead; the eyes/ lids and root of the nose; and the lower face, including the cheeks, mouth, most of the nose, and chin. The Facial Affect Scoring Technique (FAST) consists of a series of photographs of these three different areas of the face, each photograph keyed to one of the six emotions. As might well be expected, for each of the emotions there is more than one FAST photograph for at least one facial area. For example, for surprise there is one brow/forehead, one eyes/lids/root of nose, but four different FAST photographs of the lower face.

The next obvious question was whether FAST is correct. Are the six emotions—happiness, sadness, anger, fear, disgust, and surprise-in actuality com posed of the facial appearances listed in FAST? Or, does the FAST appearance of disgust actually occur with anger, and so forth? We have conducted four experiments on the validity of FAST. Two of the experiments attempted to prove the validity of FAST by showing that measurements of the face with FAST corresponded with other evidence of the subjective emotional experience of the persons whose faces were measured. These experiments investigated the experiential validity of FAST.

The other two experiments investigated the social validity of FAST. Rather than attempting to prove that FAST measurements correspond to the person's experience, these studies investigated whether FAST measurements can predict what observers think a person is feeling when they look at his face. Although experiential and social validity should be related, they need not necessarily be so. We may not look to others how we actually feel, at least all of the time. Thus, it was necessary to study both experiential and social validity.

The studies of experiential validity drew from materials gathered in one of the cross-cultural studies of facial expressions described earlier. College students in Japan and in the United States had individually watched pleasant and unpleasant movies while we videotaped their facial expressions. From their answers to questionnaires after the experiment, it was clear that they experienced very different emotions while watching the two types of films.

In describing their reactions to the travelogue, the subjects had said it was interesting and pleasant, and caused them to feel moderate happiness. In describing their reactions to the surgical film, the subjects said they had unpleasant, disgusted, pained, fearful, sad, and surprised feelings. If FAST is valid, then measurements based on it should be able to distinguish between the facial expressions shown when these two different sets of emotions were experienced.

All of the facial muscular movements visible on the videotapes were isolated, their duration was measured, and they were classified in terms of FAST. This measurement procedure was done in slow motion, with the measurements made separately for the three areas of the face, by three separate technicians. Such precise measurement required about five hours for each minute of videotaped facial behavior. The results were very clear-cut. Measurements with FAST clearly distinguished the two emotional conditions, whether subjects had been watching a stressful film or a travelogue. And, FAST was equally successful with the facial expressions of Japanese subjects and with Americans, as it should be, since it was built to show the universal facial expressions of emotion.

One limitation of this experiment, however, is that it didn't determine whether FAST correctly depicts the facial appearances for each of the six emotions. It only shows that FAST is correct in distinguishing between unpleasant and pleasant experiences.

The second experiential validity study provided a partial remedy to this limitation. Recent research on the physiology of emotions suggests that there are markedly different patterns of heart rate acceleration and deceleration with the emotions of surprise and disgust. Measures of heart rate and skin conductance had been gathered on the Japanese and American subjects when they were watching the pleasant and stressful films. If FAST is correct in what it says a surprise face and a disgust face look like, then when FAST says such facial expressions occurred, there should be a different pattern of heart rate for each. When we examined the changes in heart rate which coincided with facial expressions FAST had designated as either surprise or disgust, the results showed the predicted difference.

Although this second study does provide evidence of the validity of FAST for surprise and disgust, it doesn't show that FAST is necessarily valid in what it says about the other emotions-anger, happiness, sadness, fear. Since FAST was derived by the same method for all six emotions, this evidence on surprise and disgust is encouraging about the likelihood that similar evidence could be obtained for the other emotions.

How are facial expressions controlled?

How can we tell a real facial expression of emotion from a simulated one? When a person doesn't feel the way he looks but is attempting to mislead us about his feelings is there any way to detect his real feelings in his facial expression? In short, does the face "leak?"

We have been studying this problem for a number of years. We started with films of the facial expressions of psychiatric patients during interviews. In certain interviews we knew from subsequent events that the patients had been misleading the interviewer about their feelings. Study of these films provided the basis for a theory of nonverbal *leakage*, ways to tell from facial expression or body movement, feelings the person was attempting to conceal. We have been testing this theory during the last five years by studying interviews in which one person purposefully conceals from another the negative emotions experienced as a result of watching very unpleasant stressful movies. The subjects in this experiment try to convince the interviewer that the film they have seen was actually pleasant and that they enjoyed it.

Our studies of these interviews are far from complete. We do know that untrained observers who look at the face are fooled, they cannot tell the honest from the deceptive interactions. We have also found that people who have been trained with the Facial Action Coding System can detect deception, but the number of people who have done this is too small to place much confidence in this result. We have developed a theory on exactly how to detect deception in facial expression, but it will take another few years to test by measuring expression with the Facial Action Coding System.

Individual differences in facial expression

In the last few years we have been developing theory and conducting experiments on how personality may be manifest in facial behavior. It would be premature to attempt here more than a brief description of our approach to this phenomenon. We believe that some of the individual differences in facial behavior result from idiosyncracies in the learning of display rules.

Display rules are social norms regarding facial appearance, probably learned early in life and functioning on a habitual basis. They specify which one of four management techniques is to be applied by whom to which emotion in a given circumstance. The four management techniques are :(1) to intensify, (2) to deintensify, (3) to neutralize the appearance of a felt emotion, or (4) to mask it with the facial configuration of another emotion. For example, at a United States white middle-class wedding display rules specify that the groom must mask any appearance of distress or fear with a happy countenance, while the bride is not similarly constrained. Another example of a display rule is that, in a patient-physician encounter the patient, no matter what the illness, must in the initial greeting reciprocate the physician's (also required) smile, before facially displaying negative affect relevant to the illness. We believe that psychotic—depressives fail to follow this display rule and, unlike neurotic—depressives, will not as often show the initial greeting smile. We also believe that the later appearance of the greeting smile is correlated with a sign of improvement in mental state. More generally, the psychotic—depressive patient fails to follow the usual display rules regarding the management of negative affect.

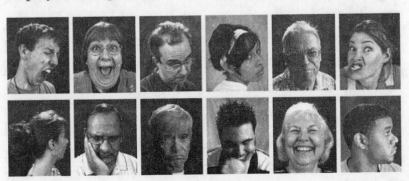

It is not that psychotic—depressed patients are unique in the facial appearance they show with negative affects but in their consistently maintained negative affect across situations and their seeming inability to modulate it. Put in other terms, in the depressed patient certain negative affects are *flooded*.

We believe that, as a result of particular display rules learned within the family, individuals may in their adult life show *blocks* in facial affect expression. In the extreme, the person may be *poker-faced,* never revealing in his face how he feels. A less extreme deviation is the block in expressing a particular emotion; for example, a person may never facially show anger. A lesser deviation is the block in the expression of a particular emotion toward a particular class of people. For example, the person may never show anger toward female authority figures. From a pilot study, it appears that blocks in expression may be manifest in two rather different ways.

One is that the person simply does not show the facial expression of a felt emotion. In a more complex manifestation, the expression is not blocked but the feedback is, such that the person is remarkably unaware of having shown the particular expression.

We believe it may also be possible to characterise people in terms of an extraordinary facility for showing emotional expressions in their faces. For some, this may be characteristic of all the emotions, and they may get into trouble or at least be known for showing everything in their face. The facility may, however, be more specific to a particular emotion, so that the person often looks afraid or angry, and so forth. A neighbouring concept, first described by Silvan Tomkins, is that of the *frozen* affect. The frozen affect is an enduring muscular set of the face; after a particular expression, the face, instead of returning to a neutral countenance, may return to a slight version of one or another affect. Thus, the person always looks just slightly disgusted or amused or melancholy, etc.

Another manifestation of personality may be in affect blends and affect sequences. In an affect *blend*, the face shows the distinctive characteristics of two emotions simultaneously.

While it is possible for any given event to elicit two emotions simultaneously, resulting in a blend expression, individuals may show a blend when only one emotion has been elicited by an external event, if they have an established habit of associating a second feeling with the elicited one. For example, when disgust is aroused, some people may characteristically feel also afraid of being disgusted; others may feel angry; others may feel happy and so forth. This affect-about-the-affect will repetitively be manifest in either a blend or a rapid sequence of the two emotions in the face.

It should be clear that what has been said so far about

individual differences in facial expressions of emotion is based on either pilot studies or hunch and still enjoys more the status of conjecture than formalized hypothesis. Yet these kinds of phenomena are now amenable to systematic investigation. Research on personality differences and facial behavior has been stymied by the lack of any systematic, quantitative procedure for measuring the spontaneous facial expressions of emotion.

However, the Facial Action Coding System described earlier provides the investigator with one necessary tool for quantifying the moment- to-moment changes that may occur in facial behaviour.

The approach to the study of individual differences discussed so far has entailed the investigation of the encoding of emotion. It is also possible to study how individuals differ in their decoding of the facial expressions of others. Personality and psychopathology may be manifest, for example, not just in a patient's blocks in the facial expression of certain emotions, but in blocks in his sensitivity to or understanding of the facial expressions of others.

We have begun a series of experiments on individual differences in the decoding of facial expression of emotion. We have developed a test which we call the Brief Affect Recognition Test (BART), which measures a person's accuracy in decoding six emotions—happiness, sadness, anger, fear, disgust, and surprise. The test employs still photographs of facial expressions that, when seen for five seconds, elicit very high agreement about the presence of one or another of these emotions. In the test we present these faces in a tachistoscope, with an exposure ranging from .01 to .04 sec. Our rationale for such a brief presentation is that it approximates usual interpersonal conditions, in which a single facial expression can easily be missed. The usual facial expression lasts only 1 or 2 sec, is embedded in preceding and subsequent facial behavior, and competes for attention with body movement, voice quality, and verbal content.

Our hypothesis is not that people will differ in their total performance, that is, in their accurate recognition of all six emotions, but that they will differ in their patterns of accuracy, recognising three or four emotions and not the others. Two studies have been completed.

One experiment compared medical patients, schizophrenics, and depressives. No difference was found in total accuracy; as predicted, depressives were less accurate on fear, whereas schizophrenics were less accurate on disgust. In the second experiment, we found that subjects who had ingested marijuana performed differently from those who had ingested alcohol; moreover, there was a relationship between self-reported mood and accuracy in recognising particular emotions. We are currently attempting to replicate these findings and standardise the BART.

Other investigators have also been interested in individual differences in facial expression, relating the ability to understand emotion in others to whether or not the person typically shows emotion in his own face. The tasks used to measure understanding of emotion and expressiveness has varied across investigators, and so have the results. As yet the contradictions have not been resolved.

Conclusion

Progress has been made in the study of facial expressions. Some of the emotions that can be shown in the face have been identified. Evidence has been accumulated to show that it is possible to read facial expression accurately. The universality of certain aspects of facial expression has been shown. Some of the precise muscular configurations that signify particular emotions have been isolated. Also, it has been shown that facial expression can fool at least some people when deception is occurring.

Despite this progress, knowledge about facial expression is still quite limited. Little is known about the differences between felt and phony expressions. While it is clear that individuals differ in facial expressiveness and in how well they understand the facial expressions of others, little is known about how this operates and how it is related to personality.

There are a number of other aspects of facial expression not touched upon here. Little is known about the early development of facial expression in the infant. Equally sparse is the information about how facial expression is related to other physiological measures that change with emotional arousal. What of the relationship between the facial muscles and the skeletal muscles; what is the relationship between what people do with their face and body? There is no reason to leave out the voice and words, and we can ask how facial expressions of emotion relate on a moment-to-moment basis with speech. This leads directly into study of the role and function of facial expression in interaction, examining how the facial expressions of one person interrelate with the facial expressions of another. There is much work for the next decade of research on facial expression.

7

Body Language in Business

It is an amazing fact that body language accounts for over 90% of a conversation. Body language can be used to help conduct an interview, give a presentation or make that important sale: a conversation stretches so much further than speech. Body language is the reason why selling face-to-face has a huge advantage over selling by phone.

Usually when we communicate with or see people, we only respond to what is being said, heard or generally seen. There is so much more involved and most of us do not pick up on it: it's our body language and it can express a thousand words. Our body language will give others an impression of ourselves or show our emotions.

Our body language is an important aspect of running a successful business as we cannot always say what we really feel. This means we have to act positive in negative situations (and vice-versa of course). You can also identify other people's body language and know what they really mean: whatever they may be saying.

You may immediately think of this as standing tall and up right as much as possible. In fact, it is the natural alignment of your head and body without the use of tension and 'locking'.

Everyone has a different posture and it usually develops through habit over the years. This may be slumping your shoulders forward or hanging your head: anything that has come to feel natural.

Your posture may show how you will approach a situation. For example, if you stand with your shoulders hanging, arms folded, and leaning to one side, it will look as if you aren't ready for or interested in the task in question. Should you stand with strong shoulders, head up, arms out by the side and closed fists, you will look as if you are ready for anything no matter how much stress is involved.

Looking at a persons feet when they are sitting down will tell you who is an extrovert (out-going) and who is an introvert (withdrawn). Extrovert – toes pointing out, introvert – toes pointing in.

The space around you

Those who stand always look more powerful to those people who are sitting down. This is because they are taking up more space. So if you feel comfortable standing, use it to look as though you have a higher status then those around you.

When you move around, the more space you take up can make others seem threatened by your presence. This is because those around you may feel that their presence in the area is less significant. In such case, they may move around using as little space as possible.

If you are sitting, you can still give an image of power. If standing isn't appropriate, use more space by stretching your legs out or by having your arms at the side of the chair. When you are on the phone and you need to be assertive, standing up will project your urgency.

Hand-to-face movements

Look out for customers that use hand-to-face movements such as holding their chin or scratching their face. This can usually show that they are thinking of making a purchase but they have a concern, for example, "can I afford it" or "what if I pick the wrong size", etc.

This may be a cue for you to move in before they leave and inform them that they can 'buy on credit if preferred' or that they can 'exchange the product if it is not suitable', etc. It is a fact that many customers do not ask to solve their queries and therefore leave if they are unsure: this is why it is important to recognise this common form of body language.

Gestures

Doing one thing may mean another as the case may be. These are things that we should look out for, as it can easily give things away about both yourself and the observer. A simple touch of the nose could mean that you/ they aren't being truthful.

A lot of us move our heads when we are talking to get approval from others. If you want to look powerful, then you should try to keep your head movements to a minimum.

How much you show your underbelly (your front) is a way of showing how confident, secure or trusting you are. The less you cover up your underbelly with folding arms, crossed legs, raised hands, etc, the more appropriate the qualities may be. Folding your arms may look as if you are trying to defend yourself and will look bad to the other person.

If you talk to someone who originally has folded arms, crossed legs and perhaps turning away slightly, you may think that they are uninterested and also feeling detached from your conversation. If they start to unfold their arms, uncross their legs, etc, it may be a sign that they are accepting your issue.

Another gesture that we use is called 'mirroring'. You may not know it, but we are attracted to those people who are similar to ourselves. A case may be where you are with an employee to discuss an issue and you both take a similar sitting/standing position. The discussion goes well, but if you had taken a different position, it may not have gone as well as it did. This gesture is often taken on by sales people who sit in a similar position as their customer.

A more common gesture is perhaps the one that is most annoying. It is known as 'displacement activity' and is used to get rid of physical tension in the body. Examples of this may include nail-biting, playing with hair, chewing gum, and teeth grinding.

Grooming gestures are those things we do to reassure ourselves. This may involve you perfecting your hair or fiddling with your clothes. We normally do this when we are around people we don't know, and so we groom ourselves to make us look more presentable to lift our confidence.

Finally, our hands are used to emphasize what we say, from pointing and saying "over there", to waving someone away and saying "go away". Hands that are made into a pyramid shape (fingers and thumbs on both hands touching, with palms wide apart) mean power. If someone sitting across a desk from you talks to you with the pyramid gesture pointing to you, this will either be your boss, or your future boss!

Negotiation skills

Negotiation is something that we do all the time and is

not only used for business purposes. For example, we use it in our social lives perhaps for deciding a time to meet, or where to go on a rainy day. Negotiation is usually considered as a compromise to settle an argument or issue to benefit ourselves as much as possible.

Communication is always the link that will be used to negotiate the issue/argument whether it is face-to-face, on the telephone or in writing. Remember, negotiation is not always between two people: it can involve several members from two parties. There are many reasons why you may want to negotiate and there are several ways to approach it. The following is a few things that you may want to consider.

Why Negotiate?

If your reason for negotiation is seen as 'beating' the opposition, it is known as 'Distributive negotiation'. This way, you must be prepared to use persuasive tactics and you may not end up with maximum benefit. This is because your agreement is not being directed to a certain compromise and both parties are looking for a different outcome.

Should you feel your negotiation is much more 'friendly' with both parties aiming to reach agreement, it is known as 'Integrative negotiation'. This way usually brings an outcome where you will both benefit highly.

Negotiation, in a business context, can be used for selling, purchasing, staff (e.g. contracts), borrowing (e.g.

loans) and transactions, along with anything else that you feel are applicable for your business.

Planning and how to negotiate

Pre-Negotiation

Before you decide to negotiate, it is a good idea to prepare. What is it exactly that you want to negotiate? Set out your objectives (e.g. I want more time to pay off the loan). You have to take into account how it will benefit the other party by offering some sort of reward or incentive.

What is involved (money, sales, time, conditions, discounts, terms, etc)? Know your extremes: how much extra can you afford to give to settle an agreement? Although you are not aiming to give out the maximum, it is worth knowing so that you will not go out of your limits.

Know what your opposition is trying to achieve by their negotiation. This is useful information that could be used to your benefit and may well be used to reach a final agreement.

Consider what is valuable to your business, not the costs. You may end up losing something in the negotiation that is more valuable to your business than money. It could be a reliable client or your company reputation.

Negotiating

It is important that you approach the other party directly to make an appointment to negotiate should it be in person, writing or by phone (not through a phone operator, receptionist, assistant etc) as this will allow you to set the agenda in advance, and improve the prospects of the other party preparing sufficiently enough to make a decision on the day. Try to be fairly open about your reason for contact or they may lose interest instantly and not follow up on the appointment. Save all your comments for the actual appointment – don't give away anything that will give them a chance to prepare too thoroughly: it's not war, but it is business!

So, it's time to negotiate and you've prepared well. What else must you have? Two things: confidence and power. Your power will come from your ability to influence. For example, you may be the buyer (but not always a strong position), or have something that the other party wants, or you may be able to give an intention to penalize if the other party fails to meet the agreement (as is the way with construction). You may be able to give a reward or an incentive. For example, you may be selling kitchen knives and as part of the package you are giving a knife sharpener and a storage unit away free as an incentive.

It is always important that you keep the negotiation in your control: this can mean within your price range, your delivery time or your profit margin. If you fail to do so, you will end up on the wrong side of the agreement, and with nothing more out of the deal other than maintaining trading relationships.

When negotiating, aim as high as you feel necessary in order to gain the best deal for yourself. The other party may bring this down but it is a good tactic, as it is always easier to play down than to gain.

Make sure that you remain flexible throughout the negotiation in case the opposition decides to change the direction of the agreement (they may want different incentives or even change their objectives). This is where your preparation comes to good use: knowing your limits and the other party's needs. If you're a quick thinker then you've got an advantage. You'll need to turn it around quickly if things start to go against you without putting your objectives at risk.

Confidence comes from knowing your business, your product, what its worth, and being able to communicate this well to the other party: these people are almost impossible to get the better of, as some of you will know only too well.

Business Body Language: Handshakes, Eye Contact, Posture, and Smiles

Your body language, i.e., your demeanour, impacts your success. It's vital that you know how to act when you get to a conference, after-hours, meeting or trade show to make the most effective and efficient use of your time ... and to attract those people whom you want to do with

business with and add to your network.

The success of any encounter begins the moment someone lays eyes on you. One of the first things they notice about you is your aura, that distinctive atmosphere that surrounds you. You create it, and you are responsible for what it says about you and whom it attracts. Your aura enters with you and starts speaking long before your open your mouth. Since body language conveys more than half of any message in any face-to-face encounter, how you act is vital to your aura.

1) Posture

One of the first key things people notice is how you carry and present yourself. Do you walk and stand with confidence like your mother taught you?

- Stomach in
- Chest out
- Shoulders back
- Head up

Or do you slouch, perhaps with your shoulders drooping, your head forward and your stomach protruding? Are you saying to people that you are not sure of yourself, are not poised and, therefore, not the one they should seek out and get to know? You may be turning people away without even being aware of it.

Command respect by standing tall and claiming the space to which you are entitled. Plant your feet about six to eight inches apart with one slightly in front of the others. My workshop attendees always remark about how this positioning makes them feel "grounded," "rooted" and "balanced" ... great ways to start any encounter!

You also tell people through your posture if you are want others to approach you. For instance, if you are talking with one other person and the two of you are forming a rectangle, you will give the message that you have "closed off" your space and don't want to be interrupted. If you doubt me, stand by two people who are in the rectangular position and see how long you go unacknowledged. The two will see you out of their peripheral vision, but won't include you until they have finished their "private" conversation. If, on the other hand, the two of you stand with your feet pointed outward like two sides of an incomplete triangle, you will be inviting others into the conversation. You can make that all-important eye contact.

2) Handshakes

Another vital component you need to bring to any interpersonal encounter is a firm handshake. Again, those few seconds you "shake" can empower or weaken a relationship. Men's handshakes are typically strong and firm because they naturally have a stronger grip.

Women, get a grip and be noticed! I once got a client

because the man I shook hands with remarked about my strong handshake and asked what I did. He decided it was time to hire me to teach his people how to shake hands, too!

Being familiar with the following handshakes will help you immensely in your relationship-building activities:

Controller

A person extends his hand to you, web-to-web, and as soon as your hands are linked, he purposely maneuvers his hand onto the top. He's telling you he wants to be in charge. Keep that in mind as the interaction continues.

Sandwich

Use this one only with people you know. When you envelop another person's hands, you are invading their private space ... where you are to be only when invited. Society promotes the standard handshake but is not as tolerant of using both hands. By the way, this handshake is also known as the politician's handshake ... which may be cause enough for most people to avoid it!

Dead fish

Imagine rubbing a scaly, dead fish in your hands ... and you got the picture. Your hands typically are wet for two reasons: You are nervous or you have been holding a cold beverage in your right hand and move it to your left just before you shake hands. In either case, it is extremely unpleasant for the receiver. If you experience anxiety, wipe your hands on a napkin, the tablecloth or even lightly on your clothes. What you spend at the dry cleaners will be paid for quickly by the better impression you make. As for the beverage, use common sense.

Limp fingers

Women, far more than men, extend their fingers rather than their entire hand. It can be painful for the extender, when she is greeted by a man who shakes with his forceful grip. Men tell me this frequently leads to their giving women a lighter handshake. Professional women respond that they want to be treated equally. One of the ways to combat this syndrome is to always extend you full hand (never cup it) horizontally, even if your grip is light.

Ingredients of a good handshake

- Hold the person's hand firmly.
- Shake web-to-web, three times maximum.
- Maintain constant eye contact.
- Radiate positive aura.

3) Eye contact

Make it and keep it! Not only does focused eye contact display confidence on your part, it also helps you understand what the other person is really saying verbally.

When the eyes say one thing, and the tongue another, a practiced man relies on the language of the first.

–Ralph Waldo Emerson

Looking someone in the eye as you meet and talk with him/her also shows you are paying attention. Listening is the most important human relations skill, and good eye contact plays a large part in conveying our interest in others.

When to look

Begin as soon as you engage someone in a conversation. However, you may wish to start even earlier if you are trying to get someone's attention. Continue it throughout the conversation. Be sure to maintain direct eye contact as you are saying "good-bye." It will help leave a positive, powerful lasting impression.

Where to look

Imagine an inverted triangle in your face with the base of it just above your eyes. The other two sides descend from it and come to a point between your nose and your lips. That's the suggested area to "look at" during business conversations. Socially, the point of the triangle drops to include the chin and neck areas. When people look you "up and down," it's probably mor==e than business or a casual social situation they have in mind!

How long to look

I suggest about 80-90 percent of the time. Less than that can be interpreted as discomfort, evasiveness, lack of confidence or boredom. When you stare longer, it can be construed as being too direct, dominant or forceful and make the other person uncomfortable. It's okay to glance down occasionally as long as your gaze returns quickly to the other person. Avoid looking over the other person's shoulders as if you were seeking out someone more interesting to talk with.

4) Smiles

Smiles are an important facial expression. They show interest, excitement, empathy, concern; they create an upbeat, positive environment. Smiles can, however, be overused. Often, men smile when they are pleased; women smile to please. You know which is the most powerful!

To gain and increase respect, first establish your presence in a room, then smile. It is far more professional than to enter a room giggling or "all smiles."

8

Importance of Effective Body Language

Effective body language supports the message and projects a strong image of the presenter. Audiences respond best to presenters whose bodies are alive and energetic. Audiences appreciate movement when it is meaningful and supportive of the message. The most effective movements are ones that reflect the presenter's personal investment in the message.

Anyone can utter a series of words; it is the presenter's personal connection to those words that can bring them to life for the audience. Presenters who care deeply about their material tends to use their entire bodies to support the message. Their gestures are large enough to embrace the room full of people. They stand tall and lean into the audience right from their feet, as if trying to shorten the distance between their message and the ears of the audience. Their faces express their passion while their eyes connect with the audience, focusing on one person at a time.

Communicating effectively means more than knowing what to say and when to say it. Communication involves the subtle signals your body language sends to those listening. Here are some common body actions and the impressions they create:

- *Fiddling* – Playing with your watch or a pen looks like you're bored or impatient

- *Clock watching* – It looks like you're anxious to move on to something else.

- *Tapping* – Tapping your foot or fingers suggests you are impatient or nervous.

- *Staring* – An unblinking stare conveys aggression

- *Legs crossed or body hunched* – Closing up your body profile — becoming smaller — looks like you lack confidence.

- *Arms crossed* – If you keep your arms folded during communication, you appear to be defending yourself against the others.

- *Touching your face* – When you have your hand in front of your mouth, you appear timid.

- *Rubbing your nose, looking away* – People who are lying often rub their nose or look away when speaking.

- *No eye contact* – If you won't look the other speaker in the eye, you seem to have low interest or a lack of confidence.

How you say things in communication is just as important as what you say. Watch your body language and control the unconscious message you might be sending.

Here is a look on some right gestures, stance and facial expressions which are very important in making an impressive statement.

Gesture

Do use your hands. They don't belong on your hips or in your pockets or folded across your chest either or held behind your back. Use them-to help emphasize a point, to express emotion, to release tension, and to engage your audience.

Most people have a gestural vocabulary at their disposal. Anyone can all think of a gesture that supports words such as "short" or "tall;" however, the gestures of everyday conversation tend to be too small and often too low to use in front of a large audience. Presenters need to scale their gestures to the size of the room. The most effective gestures arise from the shoulder, not the wrist or elbow. Shoulder gestures project better across the distance and release more of the presenter's energy, helping combat any tension that can build in the upper body (particularly under pressure).

Stance

How you stand in front of the room speaks before open your mouth. Your stance can tell the audience that you're happy, scared, confident, or uncomfortable. Audiences "read" these messages unthinkingly but unfailingly. Stance speaks. A balanced stance with weight even but slightly forward tends to say that the speaker is engaged with the audience. A slumped stance leaning to one side can says the speaker doesn't care.

The feet should point straight ahead, not quite shoulder-width apart. When not gesturing, the hands should sit quietly at the sides of the presenter. Letting the hands fall to the sides between gestures projects ease. These moments of stillness between gestures also have the effect of amplifying the gestures. Yes, you can move around, but remember to punctuate that movement with stillness. Constant motion, such as swaying, is a distraction that can annoy your listeners.

Facial expression

The movements of your eyes, mouth, and facial muscles can build a connection with your audience. Alternatively, they can undermine your every word. Eye focus is the most important element in this process. No part of your facial expression is more important in communicating sincerity and credibility. Nothing else so directly connects you to your listeners-whether in a small gathering or a large group. Effective presenters engage one person at a time, focusing long enough to complete a natural phrase and watch it sink in for a moment. This level of focus can rivet the attention of a room by drawing the eyes of each member of the audience and creating natural pauses between phrases. The pauses not only boost attention, but also contribute significantly to comprehension and retention by allowing the listener time to process the message.

The other elements of facial expression can convey the feelings of the presenter, anything from passion for the subject, to depth of concern for the audience. Unfortunately, under the pressure of delivering a group presentation, many people lose their facial expression. Their faces solidify into a grim, stone statue, a thin straight line where the lips meet. Try to unfreeze your face right from the start. For example, when you greet the audience, smile! You won't want to smile throughout the entire presentation, but at least at the appropriate moments. It's only on rare occasions that you may need to be somber and serious throughout.

Bring it all together

While we all want to believe that it's enough to be natural in front of a room, it isn't really natural to stand up alone in front of a group of people. It's an odd and unusual thing that creates stress, tension, and stomach troubles. Being natural won't cut it. We need to be bigger, more expressive, and more powerful. It takes extra effort and energy. It also takes skill and practice. With so much depending on communication and communication depending on body language, it's worth getting it right. Work on your body language-gesture, stance, and facial expression-to make the most of every speaking opportunity.

Effective body language in meetings

Reading body language

When it is your turn to you are make a contribution, the best way of staying in control and keeping the other participants with you is to keep them interested in what you are saying. Meeting participants who are not actually speaking don't usually think of themselves as being observed. Consequently, their body language is relatively easy to read.

Body language signals that you might observe among your meeting partners include: Resistance or disagreement can be implied if you observe a negative posture, with an impassive or slightly hostile expression, arms folded as if to form a barrier and legs crossed with the person leaning back. However, you should be careful to avoid making judgments based on observing one aspect of body language in isolation. For example, crossed legs or crossed arms on their own should not automatically be read as a negative reaction. A neutral and open attitude is often accompanied by a neutral or slightly friendly facial expression and an upright or slightly forward leaning seating position.

As these people have not yet decided whether or not they agree with your main message you may observe a mixture of gentle nods and shakes of their head as you make your key points. Neutrals should be viewed as a positive resource; your main challenge is to win them over.

The ability to read body language signals will help you to judge who you have on-side, who is opposing your point of view and who has yet to decide. This should help you to focus your message where it can have maximum impact, talking round those that can be swayed, whilst keeping your supporters with you and trying not to alienate the opposition.

Encouraging interaction

In order to make your contribution clearly and concisely, it is often advisable to include a question and answer session at the end, and make this clear at the outset. This will enable you to deliver your message and then end strongly, before entering the relatively unpredictable area of tackling questions from the other participants.

When you have finished preparing your contribution, read through it carefully, this is the time to focus on any areas in which your message is short of facts or vulnerable to being challenged. It is often possible to anticipate most questions that are likely to arise. When answering questions do so by speaking clearly and confidently, otherwise you will appear unsure of what you are saying. Don't let nerves draw you into responding hastily, always think about your answer before you speak and if necessary refer back to your notes in order to answer a question. If the question requires clarification then ask the questioner to do this, rather than risk answering a question that wasn't asked. When answering, address the entire meeting and not just to the questioner. Avoid getting into a protracted debate on any point that is raised. You may offer to see a questioner after the meeting to continue a point that is of specific interest to them alone.

Four main aspects

You need to be aware of your body language from the moment you begin to make your contribution to the meeting. The other participants will analyse your body language, even if they are unaware of this at the conscious level. A brilliantly prepared presentation delivered in an interesting voice will often fail to be convincing if it is accompanied by negative, intrusive or hostile body language. There are four main aspects of body language that you should consider; what to do with your eyes, what your facial expressions indicate, the positioning and movement of your body and limbs, and your hand gestures.

Positive eye contact

Eye contact is an essential part of any communication. Without it people are unlikely to relate to the message in a meaningful way. Not many people realize how important eye contact is, or how sensitive people are to it. Eye contact should be a positive form of body language communication, but if it is not used correctly it can easily become negative.

The face shown has a shaded area, which indicates the correct target zone for positive eye contact. Looking anywhere within this shaded zone represents positive eye contact. Think about where else you might be tempted to look at someone's face during a conversation or presentation. Which area of the face do you think would cause the most discomfort to the person being looked at? Looking at someone's face anywhere outside of the triangular target zone is likely to cause some degree of embarrassment. However, the two no-go zones shown are both associated with strong adverse reactions.

Zone A represents the intimate zone and by moving just a fraction below the base of the target triangle you will enter it. When this happens people typically react by feeling that the other person is staring at them, or that the observer looks shifty.

Zone B represents a dominant zone and by looking at the forehead of another person you are likely to invoke a reaction that you appear to be arrogant, that you are staring straight through them or more commonly that you are talking down at them.

As well as understanding how to make positive eye contact with an individual, in a meeting it is also important to ensure that your gaze encompasses all of the attendees.

If you do end up looking at only one or two members of a group, they are likely to feel awkward whilst the others may begin to wonder if they need to be there at all. Whilst you may find it more difficult to engage members of the group who appear neutral or even hostile, it is important to include them, as you will often need to win them over.

Body language and stance

If your meeting involves standing up to make your contribution, then you should be aware that basic aspects of your stance can easily communicate subconscious messages – some of which you will want to avoid. The sort of messages that your stance may convey include:

The forward sloping

This stance indicates a wish to dominate others. Often this stance is accompanied by an over-stressed point. The speaker may be attempting to impose a concept or point of view on their audience. This is made worse by aggressive or intrusive behaviour – such as the use of hostile gestures.

The backward sloping

This stance indicates a speaker who is not happy with their situation. This defensive or submissive stance tends to indicate that they lack confidence in what they are saying and would rather not be there.

A bent posture is indicative of a person who is saying something without conviction. Saying one thing whilst meaning another – such as a salesperson giving an exaggerated sales pitch or a customer who wants to say no but has been placed in an awkward position. The upright posture demonstrates adult, assertive behavior with no hidden meaning or manipulations in the communication.

This stance indicates that you have conviction and confidence in what you are saying. This is the posture you should practice and use when making your contribution at meetings. If you are going to be speaking for any length of time then move to the front of the room. This will make it easier for all of the participants to concentrate on your message and enables you to gauge their reaction to what you are saying.

Using body language to defuse angry people

During a hostile confrontation, a person may display aggressive body language without even thinking about it. But just as a person conveys anger through nonverbal cues, we can train ourselves to promote peace through other nonverbal cues that express peacefulness.

It is estimated that majority of human communication is not conveyed through the spoken word. The major communication is done through nonverbal communication and the vocal qualities of speech.

During a hostile confrontation between two people, both parties will naturally assume either defensive or aggressive nonverbal behaviour without even thinking about it. These aggressive nonverbal cues include, but are not limited to:

- Finger pointing (very aggressive)
- Glaring
- Invasion of personal or even intimate space (4 and closer)
- Arms crossed
- Widening of stance
- Hands on hips
- Fingers clenched into a fist
- Increase in the volume of voice

Is it possible to use nonverbal communication to defuse an angry person? The answer is: yes, it is possible. In much the same way a person conveys anger through nonverbal cues, we can also train ourselves to promote peace through nonverbal cues that express peacefulness.

Open palms

The single biggest nonverbal gesture that conveys peace is by placing your palms up so that they are facing upwards. Just as submissive dogs expose their throats to convey peace, our equivalent gesture is to turn our hands upwards.

This feels entirely unnatural when we are confronted with a hostile person, so it requires practice, but you can practice this during any conversation. Open palms not only convey submissiveness, but also honesty.

Triangle body pointing

When someone becomes angry at us, it is common for

them to turn their body so that it is directly facing our own. They might even start invading our personal space to increase their intimidation level. If we are also angry, the tendency is not to back down to this invasion, but rather meet them head on; however, this only serves to increase the level of tension.

Instead, orient your body position at 90 degrees in relation to your partner's body in such a way that if you were to draw a line in the direction that both of you are facing, it would intersect at an imaginary third point. This is known as triangle body pointing and in a normal and friendly conversation, we do it naturally.

This type of body pointing facilitates cooperation because it provides a feeling of openness during the conversation. With our bodies at 90 degrees, it creates that imaginary third point which acts like an escape route.

When we adopt a closed position, such as when we are faced directed at a person, it has a similar effect of pushing them into a corner because there is no out except through you and this is perceived as a challenge.

Looking down

In a hostile confrontation, glaring at each other is a sign of defiance and a nonverbal challenge to each other. The glare is such a powerful nonverbal signal that it can in and of itself provoke a fight.

The reverse of that is to avert your gaze downwards.

This signifies noncombativeness and submission. By gazing downwards, you are basically telling the other person, "Hey, I'm not here to fight."

Decrease voice volume

When someone gets angry, the volume of their voice tends to increase. In response to their volume, in order for us to feel like we are the dominant being, we increase our own voice to a level just above theirs. This type of vocal competition fosters conflict.

Instead of competing with their volume, do the opposite and decrease the volume of your voice. Speak in a gentle, calm, and soothing tone. The volume level of your voice should be a few notches higher than barely audible.

This does a couple of things. First, it establishes that you are not in competition with your partner. Second, your partner wants to hear things that they can use against you in an argument. They can't respond to something that they can't hear. By decreasing the volume of your voice, you in effect, force your partner into becoming a better listener.

Head tilting

Most animals, including humans, are programmed to minimise exposure to their necks because this is a vital area that can be attacked. If you have ever witnessed two dogs attacking, they instinctively go for each other's throats. Head tilting is a peaceful gesture because by tilting your head, you expose your neck. This has the psychological effect of disarming the other person by making you seem less threatening.

By using one or a combination of these nonverbal cues, you can increase your chances of defusing a direct one-on-one confrontation with another person.

9

Ways of Improving Body Language

As has been described already that body language plays an important part in making a statement about an individual. We're always taught to improve our words. We learn to improve our language and words to impress.

We learn to construct clever chains of words to gain an upper hand and to communicate more clearly. But when we grow up we learn very little beyond improving our words. In brief, once again a look on some of the important reasons why one has to improve body language.

Words are only 7 per cent of your communication

The rest is your voice tonality (38 per cent) and your body language at 55 per cent. That's according to a latest research. These numbers may vary depending upon the situation and what is communicated (for instance, talking over the phone is obviously different from talking face to face) but body language is a very important part of communication.

Increase your attractiveness

It's not what you say, it's how you say it. A better posture, a more open body language, a more controlled and focused body language will make everyone more attractive. And not just in a sexual way but when talking to new friends or in job interviews and business meetings.

Emotions are linked to your body language

Emotions work backwards too. If you feel good you'll smile. If you force yourself to smile you'll feel good too. If you feel tired or down you might sit slumped down. If you sit slumped down you'll feel more tired and negative. Just try to sit straight up for 5 minutes and feel the difference in energy from half-lying in your chair.

Reduce mixed messages

If you're in a job interview and you talk with a steady voice and say all the confident things you should but your body language tells your maybe-employers that you are very nervous or guarded then you are incongruent (and perhaps without that job). What you want is be congruent, that is for your words, your voice and your body language to say the same thing.

Improve your communication skills

If you improve your body language you can get your thoughts across in a more effective way. You can create a connection to another person more easily. When using more powerful and appropriately balanced body language your communication skills become more focused and better.

Better first impressions

Everyone stereotypes everyone on first impression, even if we are reluctant to do it. We all get a first impression of a new person that creates a mental image of his or her personality in our minds. That image of you often lasts. Having a better body language will consistently give people a more positive mental snapshot of you.

Some ways to improve body language

Show confidence through your walk and posture

Do you keep in mind that your walk and posture bespeak your confidence before you begin your pitch? They influence your audience of one or one hundred to make initial decisions about your capabilities before you even shake hands, begin a conversation or show your first slide.

The way you stride down the hallway, across the parking lot or into a room is a powerful first clue to how you feel about yourself. Walk erect with your head held high, your shoulders back, your chest out and your stomach in. With the aura you create, you command respect without ever saying a word.

When you overdo it with a swagger or a strut, it can equate with egotism and a pompous attitude. Underdone, like when you have your back arched and your head stuck out and down, shows a lack of confidence.

When you are giving a presentation, use your walk as a form of physical punctuation. Strengthen transitions by stepping to the side, pauses by standing in place and emphasis and persuasion by moving forward as if you want to touch the audience.

If your movement is unnatural or mechanical, it will detract from your presentation. Standing in one place throughout a talk may indicate you're "frozen to the spot" by the fear of speaking.

Your posture talks as well

Once you have walked into that meeting, office or conference and found your spot, your posture becomes a telltale sign. Remember what your mother used to tell you, "Stand up straight!" You literally "make your stand" through your posture. It tells people how confident you are, how much self-esteem you have and how you want to be treated.

Taking up a reasonable amount of space equates to having power. Plant your feet about 8 to 10 inches apart with one slightly in front of the other. This allows you to easily change weight from one foot to the other. This is particularly important if you are behind a podium; you don't noticeably appear to be shifting weight (which you need to do so you don't get frozen in the "speaker" position). When you don't do it smoothly, this shifting can be distracting to the audience and to you when you become conscious of it.

This stance also makes you feel more comfortable, balanced and grounded, which is a plus when you undertake the arduous process of starting or maintaining a conversation.

Women often think it is more ladylike to assume the first position in ballet, i.e. the inside back of your left foot rubs against the inside arch of your right foot. In reality, women who stand in this position in business look as if they might topple if given a nudge.

Avoid the fig-lead stance

A stance to avoid is what we term the fig leaf. In addition to having your feet close together and your hands crossed over your genital area, you may tilt your head sideways as you look up to engage in conversation. This posture almost always guarantees you a loss of respect and power before you ever say a word!

How to achieve good posture

- Stand with your back to a wall and look straight ahead. Make sure your head and your back are touching the wall. As you remain standing there for a few minutes, periodically touch your shoulders to the wall and hold for 10 seconds.

This automatically makes you pull in your tummy and stick out your chest. Take a few steps away from the wall, and practice the same techniques on your own.

- Now, stand up. Imagine your body is a tall, narrow building. Plant your feet 8-10 inches apart.

  Now, make sure your knees are directly about your feet, hips above your knees, stomach above your hips, chest above your stomach and head above your chest – such that if you took a piece of heavy string and dropped it from your nose, it would fall between your feet. Keep this image in mind as you stand around at networking events, meetings and receptions.

Improving body language while speaking in public

When speaking in public, paying too much attention to your every gesture and body movement could detract from your message rather than enhancing it. Some people may advice that to show union, interlace the fingers in front of the body. To indicate separation, make a chopping motion across an upturned palm. To convey power, clench your fist and so on. Unfortunately, such advice, if taken to heart, can make the speaker look robotic and even ridiculous. The novice speaker might mistakenly believe that if he can manage to control his body language, he will look confident and poised and no one will notice his nerves or worse yet, no one will notice that he really doesn't have much to say. Think again.

Most people rarely focus on how they hold their body when speaking casually. Yet, put an inexperienced speaker on the platform and he immediately wonders what to do with his hands, arms, legs-how to stand, handle his props and move about the stage.

Yes, body language is important. Get it wrong and your audience will focus on your movement, not your message. But to approach public speaking from the outside in, mask over message, will only make matters worse. You'll look phony and wooden, a caricature of yourself.

We have seen some of the least polished, untrained speakers give incredible presentations. Why? Because they spoke the truth and their intention was pure. And we've all seen well-trained politicians and executives give presentations with "perfect" technique yet look like fools. Why? Because the lesser (our gestures) must serve the greater (our message), and not the other way around.

If you've ever taken a public speaking class where the presentations, were videotaped you've probably noticed that just about everyone has habits and mannerisms about which they are unaware.—hair twirling, distracting eye movements, rocking back and forth, um's , uh's and so forth. It can be quite shocking to see how unaware we are of ourselves and most people resist being videotaped.

Now the question arises that why is this so? Psychoanalysts write to answer this question that "We think consciousness, the perception of our problems, is dangerous." Yet consciousness, although we resist it the most, is our most precious asset. Awareness, even of something negative and embarrassing, is the first step to correcting our mistakes and perfecting our skills.

That being said, what makes a well-prepared speaker suddenly go wooden on stage?

Stepping into the public eye is a consciousness raising experience. We are flooded with awareness of the audience and of ourselves. Accepting this awareness is vital to the speaker. We need that feedback loop to tell us if we are making contact with the audience or not and how we must adjust ourselves to get the message across.

A wooden posture and unnatural body language is an indication that the speaker is trying to hide the awareness of his imperfections behind an overly perfect delivery, a futile attempt. What we try to hide only becomes larger and everyone sees it but us.

When you have to give a talk, align yourself with goodness, truth and beauty first. Pay attention to who you are on the inside and then attend to the external details — where you put your hands, how you stand and so on. In speaking, as in life, don't give the inferior more attention than it deserves.

Other important ways of improving body language

Improving your body language can make a big difference in your people skills, attractiveness and general mood. Here is just a few of many pointers on how to improve your body language.

There is no specific advice on how to use your body language. What you do might be interpreted in several ways, depending on the setting and who you are talking to. You'll probably want to use your body language differently when talking to your boss compared to when you talk to a girl/guy you're interested in. These are some common interpretations of body language and often more effective ways to communicate with your body.

First, to change your body language you must be aware of your body language. Notice how you sit, how you stand, how you use you hands and legs, what you do while talking to someone.

You might want to practice in front of a mirror. Yeah, it might seem silly but no one is watching you. This will give you good feedback on how you look to other people and give you an opportunity to practise a bit before going out into the world.

Another tip is to close your eyes and visualise how you would stand and sit to feel confident, open and relaxed or whatever you want to communicate. See yourself move like that version of yourself. Then try it out.

You might also want observe friends, role models, movie stars or other people you think has good body language. Observe what they do and you don't. Take bits and pieces you like from different people. Try using what you can learn from them.

Some of these tips might seem like you are faking something. But fake it till you make it is a useful way to learn something new. And remember, feelings work backwards too. If you smile a bit more you will feel happier.

If you sit up straight you will feel more energetic and in control. If you slow down your movements you'll feel calmer. Your feelings will actually reinforce your new behaviours and feelings of weirdness will dissipate.

In the beginning easy it's to exaggerate your body language. You might sit with your legs almost ridiculously far apart or sit up straight in a tense pose all the time. That's ok. And people aren't looking as much as you think; they are worrying about their own problems. Just play around a bit, practice and monitor yourself to find a comfortable balance.

Don't cross your arms or legs-You have probably already heard you shouldn't cross your arms as it might make you seem defensive or guarded. This goes for your legs too. Keep your arms and legs open.

Have eye contact, but don't stare – If there are several people you are talking to, give them all some eye contact to create a better connection and see if they are listening. Keeping too much eye-contact might creep people out. Giving no eye-contact might make you seem insecure. If you are not used to keeping eye-contact it might feel a little hard or scary in the beginning but keep working on it and you'll get used to it.

Don't be afraid to take up some space – Taking up space by for example sitting or standing with your legs apart a bit signals self-confidence and that you are comfortable in your own skin.

Relax your shoulders – When you feel tense it's easily winds up as tension in your shoulders. They might move up and forward a bit. Try to relax. Try to loosen up by shaking the shoulders a bit and move them back slightly.

Nod when they are talking – Nod once in a while to signal that you are listening. But don't overdo it and peck like Woody Woodpecker.

Don't slouch, sit up straight – But in a relaxed way, not in a too tense manner.

Lean, but not too much – If you want to show that you are interested in what someone is saying, lean toward the person talking. If you want to show that you're confident in yourself and relaxed lean back a bit. But don't lean in too much or you might seem needy and desperate for some approval. Or lean back too much or you might seem arrogant and distant.

Smile and laugh – Lighten up, don't take yourself too seriously. Relax a bit, smile and laugh when someone says something funny. People will be a lot more inclined to listen to you if you seem to be a positive person. But don't be the first to laugh at your own jokes, it makes you seem nervous and needy. Smile when you are introduced to someone but don't keep a smile plastered on your face, you'll seem insincere.

Don't touch your face – It might make you seem nervous and can be distracting for the listeners or the people in the conversation.

Keep your head up - Don't keep your eyes on the ground, it might make you seem insecure and a bit lost. Keep your head up straight and your eyes towards the horizon.

Slow down a bit – This goes for many things. Walking slower not only makes you seem more calm and confident, it will also make you feel less stressed. If someone addresses you, don't snap you're neck in their direction, turn it a bit more slowly instead.

Don't fidget – Try to avoid, phase out or transform fidgety movement and nervous ticks such as shaking your leg or tapping your fingers against the table rapidly. You'll seem nervous and fidgeting can be a distracting when you try to get something across. Declutter your movements if you are all over the place. Try to relax, slow down and focus your movements.

Use your hands more confidently – Instead of fidgeting with your hands and scratching your face use them to communicate what you are trying to say. Use your hands to describe something or to add weight to a point you are trying to make. But don't use them to much or it might become distracting. And don't let your hands flail around, use them with some control.

Lower your drink – Don't hold your drink in front of your chest. In fact, don't hold anything in front of your heart as it will make you seem guarded and distant. Lower it and hold it beside your leg instead.

Realise where your spine ends – Many people (including me until recently) might sit or stand with a straight back in a good posture. However, they might think that the spine ends where the neck begins and therefore crane the neck forward. Your spine ends in the back of your head. Keep you whole spine straight and aligned for better posture.

Don't stand too close – One of the things we learned from Seinfeld is that everybody gets weirded out by a close-talker. Let people have their personal space, don't invade it.

Mirror — Often when you get along with a person, when the two of you get a good connection, you will start to mirror each other unconsciously. That means that you mirror the other person's body language a bit. To make the connection better you can try a bit of proactive mirroring. If he leans forward, you might lean forward. If she holds her hands on her thighs, you might do the same. But don't react instantly and don't mirror every change in body language. Then weirdness will ensue.

Keep a good attitude – Last but not least, keep a positive, open and relaxed attitude. How you feel will come through in your body language and can make a major difference.

You can change your body language but as all new habits it takes a while. Especially things like keeping you head up might take time to correct if you have spent thousands of days looking at your feet. And if you try and change to many things at once it might become confusing and feel overwhelming.

Take a couple of these body language bits to work on every day for three to four weeks. By then they should have developed into new habits and something you'll do without even thinking about it. If not, keep on until it sticks. Then take another couple of things you'd like to change and work on them.

• • •